36 1993

ıford V.

ɔon

WITHDRAWN

	DATE DUE		

Siegfried Sassoon

Twayne's English Authors Series

Kinley Roby, Editor

Northeastern University

TEAS 500

SIEGFRIED SASSOON
The Bettman Archive

Siegfried Sassoon

Sanford Sternlicht

Syracuse University

Twayne Publishers • New York

Maxwell Macmillan Canada • Toronto

Maxwell Macmillan International • New York   Oxford   Singapore   Sydney

Twayne's English Authors Series No. 500

Siegfried Sassoon
Sanford Sternlicht

Twayne Publishers
Macmillan Publishing Company
866 Third Avenue
New York, New York 10022

Maxwell Macmillan Canada, Inc.
1200 Eglinton Avenue East
Suite 200
Don Mills, Ontario M3C 3N1

Library of Congress Cataloging-in-Publication Data

Sternlicht, Sanford V.
　　Siegfried Sassoon / Sanford Sternlicht.
　　　　p. cm.—(Twayne's English authors series; TEAS 500)
　　Includes bibliographical references and index.
　　ISBN 0-8057-7021-6 (alk. paper)
　　1. Sassoon, Siegfried, 1886–1967—Criticism and interpretation.
　2. Poets, English—Biography—History and criticism. 3. World War,
　1914–1918—Literature and the war. I. Title. II. Series.
　PR6037.A86Z86 1993
　a821'.912—dc20　　　　　　　　　　　　　　92-45578
　　　　　　　　　　　　　　　　　　　　　　　　CIP
　　　　　　　　　　　　　　　　　　　　　　　　AC

Contents

Preface

Although Siegfried Sassoon wrote poetry for more than 60 years, he earned his place in the history of English literature with the realistic and satiric poems he wrote relating to his experiences as a brave combat infantryman in World War I. One might say he won fame the hard way. As a poet and as a man he was remade in battle. His voice is the most authentic in the renowned chorus of the many brilliant poets who lived through or died in that horrible debacle. He became the bitter avenger of the dead and the spokesperson for sacred remembrance.

The war, his wounds, the suffering of his comrades, his courageous but futile attempt to get the British public to question the dubious attrition strategy of their generals and politicians, the cruel death of beloved friends, his experiences in a psychiatric hospital for shell-shocked victims, and his despair over the end of a way of life he loved—these led him to attempt to find solace in rewriting his prewar and wartime life again and again, especially in what is considered the greatest fictionalized account of the life of an Edwardian-gentleman-turned-warrior, the trilogy *The Complete Memoirs of George Sherston.*

Siegfried Sassoon argues against the widely held view that Sassoon's art was pure Georgian and not a part of modernism. His poetry is a landmark of twentieth-century English literature because it created a poetic language of violence that was imitated by other war poets and by British and American writers from Robert Graves and Ernest Hemingway to Dylan Thomas, Randall Jarrell, and Norman Mailer. Sassoon gave to modernism in Britain and America the subject of war realistically portrayed—like the newsreel in a "Picture-Show." The first portrait of "The Wasteland" was Sassoon's vision of no-man's-land. His war poetry was reportage raised to the level of high art in the context of actuality. His hatred for war fueled the thirties poets, especially Auden and Spender, with the message and the metaphor of pacifism. Sassoon helped to create the peace movement that flourished between the world wars, and he served it loyally and well, until Hitler's aggression made it obsolete.

Siegfried Sassoon offers a comprehensive, up-to-the-moment evaluation of the Sassoon canon and is only the second full-length study of Sassoon's contributions in poetry and prose, the first being Michael Thorpe's *Siegfried Sassoon: A Critical Study* (1967). No book-length biography of

Sassoon has been published to date, and so the Twayne *Siegfried Sassoon* contains the most accurate and comprehensive life of the poet currently available. This study is the first to include the new information made available by the publication of Sassoon diaries in the 1980s.

It is a pleasure to acknowledge my debt to Professor Michael Thorpe's painstaking, ground-breaking study of Sassoon, mentioned earlier, and to the work of Sir Rupert Hart-Davis, Sassoon's friend, literary executor, and editor of Sassoon's war poetry, letters, and diaries, a great benefit to scholars and general readers. I thank Sir Rupert for answering my letters and clarifying biographical facts. Geoffrey Keynes's *A Bibliography of Siegfried Sassoon* (1962) has been my constant companion through the labyrinthian paths of Sassoon's privately published works.

I am also grateful to many at Syracuse University, especially my excellent research assistants, Joan Pierce and Merissa Mims, and the kind, patient, indefatigable interlibrary staff of Bird Library.

The following have generously given permission to quote from the works of Siegfried Sassoon:

"Return of the Heroes" from *The War Poems of Siegfried Sassoon*. Copyright 1919 by William Heinemann. Used by permission of Heinemann Publishers.

From *Heart's Journey*. Copyright 1927 by Crosby Gaige; copyright 1929 by Harper and Brothers. Used by permission of HarperCollins Publishers.

From *Sequences*; first published in 1956 by Faber and Faber Ltd. From *The Path to Peace*; copyright 1960 Siegfried Sassoon. From *Collected Poems 1908–1956*; first published as *Collected Poems* in 1947; first published as *Collected Poems 1908–1956* in 1961 by Faber and Faber Ltd. From *The Road to Ruin*; first published in 1933 by Faber and Faber Ltd. Used by permission of George Sassoon.

From *Collected Poems*. Copyright 1918, 1920 by E. P. Dutton. Copyright 1936, 1946, 1947, 1948 by Siegfried Sassoon. Used by permission of Viking Penguin, a division of Penguin Books USA Inc.

Chronology

1886   Siegfried Loraine Sassoon born 8 September at Weirleigh, Matfield, in Kent. Second of three sons of Sir Alfred Ezra Sassoon and Theresa Thornycroft Sassoon.

1891   Education by private tutors. Parents separate.

1895   Father dies.

1900–1902   New Beacon School.

1902–1905   Marlborough College.

1906   *Poems.*

1906–1908   Clare College, Cambridge. Leaves without degree.

1908   *Orpheus in Diloeryum.*

1909   *Sonnets and Verses. Sonnets.*

1911   *Twelve Sonnets. Poems.*

1912   *Melodies. Hyacinth: An Idyll. An Ode for Music.*

1913   *The Daffodil Murderer. Amyntas.*

1914   Joins cavalry and is injured in riding accident.

1915   Transfers to infantry. Commissioned in Royal Welch Fusiliers and leaves for France. *Discoveries.*

1916   Awarded Military Cross. *Morning Glory. The Redeemer.*

1917   Wounded in France. Publishes "A Soldier's Declaration," protesting conduct of the war. Hospitalized for shell shock to prevent court-martial. *The Old Huntsman.*

1918   Voluntarily returns to combat. Service in Ireland, Palestine, and France. Awarded bar for Military Cross. Shot in the head and evacuated to England. *Counter-Attack. Picture-Show.*

1919   Discharged as captain. Period of recovery. *The War Poems of Siegfried Sassoon.*

1920   Speaking and reading tour of North America.

1923   *Recreations.*

1925   *Lingual Exercises for Advanced Vocabularians. Selected Poems.*

1926   *Satirical Poems.*

1927   *The Heart's Journey.*

1928   *Memoirs of a Fox-hunting Man.*

1929   Hawthornden Prize and James Tait Black Memorial Prize for *Memoirs of a Fox-hunting Man.*

1930   *Memoirs of an Infantry Officer.*

1931   D.Litt., Liverpool University. *Poems.*

1933   Marries Hester Gatty. *The Road to Ruin.*

1934   *Vigils.*

1936   Son, George, born. *Sherston's Progress.*

1937   *The Complete Memoirs of George Sherston.*

1938   *The Old Century and Seven More Years.*

1939   *On Poetry. Rhymed Ruminations.*

1940   *Poems Newly Selected 1916–1935.*

1942   *A Weald of Youth.*

1943   Separated from wife.

1945   *Siegfried's Journey 1916–1920.*

1947   Mother dies. *Collected Poems.*

1948   *Meredith.*

1950   *Common Chords.*

1951   Commander, Order of the British Empire. *Emblems of Experience.*

1953   Honorary Fellow, Clare College, Cambridge.

1954   *The Tasking.*

1956   *Sequences.*

1957   Converts to Roman Catholicism. Queen's Gold Medal in poetry.

1960   *The Path to Peace. Selected Poems* (new edition).

1961   *Collected Poems 1908–1956.*

1965   D.Litt., Oxford University.

1966   *Something about Myself. An Octave.*

1967 Dies on 1 September at Heytesbury, near Warminster, Wiltshire.

1981 *Siegfried Sassoon Diaries 1920–1922.*

1983 *Siegfried Sassoon Diaries 1915–1918.*

1985 *Siegfried Sassoon Diaries 1923–1925.*

Chapter One
"We're None of Us the Same"
A Life

Despite great dangers and severe battle wounds, Siegfried Sassoon, poet, autobiographer, warrior, pacifist, and fox-hunting English gentleman, lived to a serene old age and kept an open mind and a simple heart. The first part of his life was sheltered, coddled, physically active, sports-centered, nonintrospective, and, as a poet, dilatory and dilettante. But the violent and terrible trenches of World War I provided the alembic for pure and great poetry. Peace came quickly to the world in 1918 but slowly to a man wounded as much in soul as in body, for nothing in his youth had prepared Sassoon for the horror of hand-to-hand, man-to-man killing, and nothing in combat prepared him for the indifference the world later felt toward the great suffering inflicted on a generation of youth by emperors and kings and by politicians and generals. Thus for almost 50 years after the guns of Flanders had ceased firing, Siegfried Sassoon devoted his significant skills as a writer to vetting his own life, to preserving in print the memory of a gentle, civilized time before the "Great War," and to contemplating the existence of God. Slowly he descended from Golgotha to a serene plane of religious existentialism even as he remained for most of his life "a prisoner of war."

Family

Siegfried Loraine Sassoon was born on 8 September 1886 at his parents' country mansion, Weirleigh, in the village of Matfield, nestled in the tranquil Weald of western Kent. The large Sassoon family in England were descendants of wealthy eighteenth-century Mesopotamian Jewish merchants who migrated from Baghdad to Persia, then India, and finally Britain. A remarkable tribe, they have been called the "Eastern Rothschilds," a reference to that other dynamic Jewish dynasty with whom

I

they sometimes married.[1] Unlike the Ashkenazi or European Rothschilds, the Sassoons followed the Oriental Sephardic rites of Judaism.

The founder of the renowned Sassoon family was Sheikh Sason Ben Saleh (1750–1830). His son David Sassoon (1792–1864) eventually moved the family business under the protection of the Union Jack in Bombay. Several of his many sons opened and operated branches of the Sassoon trading company in England. A son and a grandson were knighted for philanthropy and business acumen. Siegfried's paternal grandfather, Sassoon D. Sassoon (1822–67), opened a London branch of David Sassoon and Sons, and although he was no business genius, the firm prospered. Siegfried's father, Alfred (1861–95), was born to great luxury. He eschewed "trade" and was trained as a concert violinist, but although he was given the best teachers money could employ, he never was more than a gifted amateur. Against his mother's wishes Alfred became the first Sassoon to marry a gentile. She disowned her son and ritually mourned him as dead. Nevertheless Alfred inherited a considerable fortune from his deceased father. Siegfried Sassoon would be raised within the milieu of his mother's family. He remained angry with the other Sassoons because, with few exceptions, they ostracized his family.[2] Sassoon D. Sassoon's descendants never had the vast wealth of the other branches of the family, the so-called Royal Sassoons who hobnobbed with Prince Albert, later King Edward VII, and entertained such eminent dignitaries as the Shah of Persia. The one Sassoon relative Siegfried knew well and cared for was his Aunt Rachel, a bluestocking who edited both the *Observer* and the *Sunday Times* simultaneously. Despite all, Siegfried would later acknowledge that although his mother's family, the Thornycrofts, provided the artistic talent in him and gave him his serenity, "the daemon in me is Jewish. And as a poetic spirit I have always felt myself—or wanted to be—a kind of minor prophet. I found . . . utterance in the war poems, of course."[3]

Alfred Sassoon's marriage was short and unhappy, although socially the couple were well paired. Theresa Georgiana Thornycroft came from landed gentry in Cheshire. She could trace her family back to the thirteenth century. There were three gifted sculptors in the family, including her brother Hamo, who, along with another brother, John, an eminent marine engineer, was knighted. Theresa and her two sisters were art lovers and proficient in sculpture and painting. She had studied painting with Ford Madox Brown.

The Sassoons had three sons in rapid succession: Michael in 1884, Siegfried in 1886, and Hamo in 1887. Theresa named her second son

Siegfried because of her admiration for Wagner's *Ring*. She was apparently oblivious to the fact that she named a half-Jewish child in honor of a composer who was one of the nineteenth-century's most notorious anti-Semites. As a youth Siegfried liked the name: "a lucky choice for me—as it has always made me want to be a hero" (Corrigan, 47). Later Sassoon realized that Wagner himself was not an admirable person to emulate.

Alfred Sassoon was mercurial, quick-tempered, and quite unable to settle down to family life in a country manor house. On the other hand, the country-bred Theresa loved Weirleigh, with its views of luxuriant gardens and rolling hills. She was completely at home in the idyllic setting. She had a studio to paint in, and she became a superb equestrian, passing on her skill and her love of horses to Siegfried. In 1891 Alfred bolted. He ran off with his wife's "best friend" and set up house with her in London. Theresa braved out the humiliation and pain, devoting herself to motherhood, religion, painting, and riding. She raised her sons as Anglicans. They saw their father for a few hours each week on Sunday visits, noting his ever-more-violent coughing. Siegfried was deeply affected by his parents' unhappiness. Alfred found little joy in his adultery. In 1895, only 34, he died in London of tuberculosis. The sensitive Siegfried, not yet nine, was too upset to attend his father's funeral in the Jewish Cemetery of London, but Michael and Hamo went and reported that they were completely baffled by the religion "Papa had given up . . . a long time ago" (*OC,* 37). Michael described the rabbis as "two old men in funny-looking hats [who] walked up and down saying 'jabber-jabber-jabber'" (*OC,* 36). Siegfried grieved deeply for his handsome, generous, musical, fun-loving, and lost father. He also empathized with his mother's hurt and rejection by both her husband and his family.

Education

As a child Siegfried received no formal education. As was the usual custom for the rich, he was instructed by a series of private tutors and a governess. Theresa had great expectations for this intelligent child; he was indeed her favorite, and she called him her "second self" (Corrigan, 48). Perhaps Sassoon's later difficulties in relating to or even having relationships with women stemmed from the extreme closeness and the mutual identifying of mother and fatherless child. Trying to push him to an early maturation, she gave him a copy of Coleridge's lectures on Shakespeare for his third birthday. Sassoon did not indicate that he got through Coleridge at such a precocious age, but he did read *Lamb's Tales from Shakespeare, Robinson Crusoe,* and *Diana of the Crossroads* at an early age (*OC,* 55, 60).

After recovery from the shock of his father's death, Siegfried's life settled down to a happy childhood in the Weald of Kent. He was healthy, and he loved outdoor activities and all sports, eventually excelling in cricket (which he played into his seventies), tennis, golf, riding, and, of course, fox-hunting. At age 10 he rather offhandedly decided that he was going to be a poet, and he began an intensive study of Longfellow, Shelley, and Tennyson.

Sassoon's first formal schooling occurred at the New Beacon School from 1900 to 1902. He was then sent to a distinguished public school, Marlborough College, only one step down from Eton, the educational domain of the richer Sassoons. At Marlborough Siegfried began to actually write poetry in 1902, and he joined the Rifle Corps. Evidencing a talent for piano and organ, he became the school student organist. On the playing fields the all-around boy excelled in cricket and rugby. He also began to collect books and keep monthly lists of his reading; however, his final academic report before departing from Marlborough in 1905 stated, "Lacks power of concentration; shows no particular intelligence or aptitude for any branch of his work; seems unlikely to adopt any special career" (*OC,* 212). His housemaster's parting advice was tersely admonitory: "Try to be more sensible" (*OC,* 212). But he departed for Cambridge "thinking only of cricket matches in the holidays, and wearing an Old Marlburian tie, which for me was neither more nor less than a badge of emancipation from an educational experience that I had found moderately pleasant but mentally unprofitable" (*OC,* 213).

Meanwhile Siegfried had grown into a handsome, robust, lean, six-foot-two athlete with a high forehead and an aquiline nose—a countenance that, along with a lifetime tendency to speak very softly and not look people straight in the eye, created a simultaneous and contradictory impression of friendliness and distantness. His two years at Clare College, Cambridge, in 1906–08, even after a post-Marlborough year of cramming, were aimless and disjointed. He tried studying law but soon found that he hated it. He transferred to a history curriculum, but instead of studying he read Pre-Raphaelite poetry. Mostly he golfed and sat up to the small hours of the morning composing "high principled poetry about nothing in particular" (*OC,* 233). He did not smoke or drink or study at

Cambridge. He certainly did not work for a university degree. At the end of his second year he was chucked out.

Meanwhile Sassoon's Uncle Hamo, the distinguished Royal Academy sculptor, had taken a liking to his nephew and tried to help him with his poetry career. He urged Siegfried to write a historical poem to compete for the Chancellor's Prize in poetry. Sassoon failed to win the prize, but he was serious enough about his poetry that he decided to find a printer, and at age 20 he published *Poems* (1906), anonymously and at his own expense, in an edition of 50 copies. They were circulated to friends and relatives at Christmas. By his own admission the poems lacked originality and were expressed in hopelessly hackneyed language. He did not know the meaning of the word *cliché* but he knew how to write one.

Having broken the news to his family of his unexpected departure from Cambridge, he decided to devote most of his time to writing poetry. At 21 he received an income of £500–£600 a year, a generous sum on which he could live in some comfort, especially considering that he was making his home at Weirleigh with his mother.[4] His expenses did, however, include the upkeep for four horses, a groom, and a stablehand. Still there was never the question of Sassoon's needing to be gainfully employed, which is not to say that he did not work and work hard: at poetry, cricket, horsemanship, and then war.

Apprenticeship

For the next six years Sassoon raced point to point on his favorite mount, Cockbird; hunted; and played serious golf. His new poems were dreamy, sentimental lyrics about flora and fauna and filled with Victorian and Pre-Raphaelite conventionalities. He became a devotee of Walter Pater (*WY*, 32–33). Edmund Gosse, the well-known critic and poet and a family friend, was kind enough or indebted enough to encourage Sassoon as he privately published book after book of verse. Finally and fortunately Sassoon discovered John Masefield and soon decided to write a parody of the future laureate's popular narrative poem *The Everlasting Mercy* (1911). While burlesquing Masefield for all he was worth, Sassoon came under the spell of the older poet, so that the supposed parody, *The Daffodil Murderer* (1913), turned out to be a pretty good imitation of Masefield, whose latest long narrative poem at that time was *The Daffodil Fields* (1913). Sassoon naturally sent a copy of *The Daffodil Murderer* to Gosse, who praised the long narrative and forwarded it to the Georgian anthologist Edward Marsh, whom Gosse and many others considered "the choragus of the new poets" (*WY,* 126).

Marsh befriended and encouraged Sassoon. They dined frequently in London, and the elder writer introduced Sassoon to the fashionable London literati. Finally Marsh practically ordered Sassoon to leave Weirleigh, move to London, and truly get serious about the business of writing. Early in 1914 and with great trepidation Sassoon took rooms near Marsh's in No. 1, The Raymond Buildings, Gray's Inn, where he could write poetry under the tutelage of his mentor and where the country gentleman could participate more fully in the cultural life of the capital. Later the devoted Marsh would anthologize Sassoon in *Georgian Poetry 1916–1917* and *Georgian Poetry 1918–1919,* the first of which would go a long way in establishing Sassoon's reputation as a poet.

At this time Siegfried also began to take more interest in his Sassoon heritage. Perhaps most significantly, Marsh introduced him to the most famous of the younger Georgians, Rupert Brooke. Brooke and Sassoon at first had little in common. Although they were about the same age, Brooke had been born in 1887, was much better educated, and was far more advanced as a poet. Siegfried quickly came under Brooke's literary influence, and his first war poems would imitate Brooke's patriotic "The Soldier," recalling "If I should die, think only this of me; / That there's some corner of a foreign field / That is forever England." Sassoon, the romantic poet, was waiting for a spark from heaven to fall and ignite his art. It fell as shrapnel. He was transmuted into a realist and a bitter satirist.

War

The summer of 1914 was especially beautiful in England, and it found Siegfried Sassoon bored. It was hard to write verse when the hounds were barking and straining and there was an opportunity to play serious county cricket. Although war loomed on the horizon, the thought was remote in Kent. Yet the "romance" of war held influence over Sassoon's class. Uniforms were dazzling. How glorious to ride in a troop of horses! It would all blow over, of course, but there was a chance of some good fun and adventure first. Sassoon said, "My heart was in my boots" (*WY,* 251).

On 31 July 1914 Sassoon bicycled nonstop 30 miles to Rye to enlist the next day as a private trooper in the Sussex Yeomanry. He did not try for a commission, for he was unsure of his ability to lead men. On 4 August Britain declared war, and Sassoon thought he would canter off to battle on troophorse Cockbird. Sassoon was the first of 12 of his name to join the colors. None seemed less likely to prove a hero, provoke great controversy, and become a legend.

Paul Fussell says in *The Great War and Modern Memory,* "Every war is ironic because every war is worse than expected."[5] Nothing in Sassoon's life as a wealthy and privileged upper-class gentleman prepared him for the experience of trench warfare, where "Corpses newly dead or in a life-like position broke right through morale no matter who was the observer."[6] Who indeed could have known how the technology of the machine age could mass-produce human slaughter? Who could believe that human beings could devise or accept the horrible idea of attrition, the central strategic concept of the western front? Who could have anticipated the effect of the sight of batches of helpless men being blown to pieces by mass artillery fire on concepts of manhood and courage formed in gentler Victorian times? Arthur E. Lane notes that "since his pre-war background had been leisured and pleasant, Sassoon was all the more alert to the contrasts provided by the conditions of life at the front."[7]

Sassoon did not go into battle as quickly as he expected. In cavalry training he broke his arm in a fall, and while recuperating and continuing to write poetry that he still privately published, he came to realize that mounted troops had little to do in the trench warfare that had developed in France and Belgium. Leaving troophorse Cockbird behind, he accepted a commission and officer training in a distinguished infantry regiment, the Royal Welch Fusiliers. Arriving in France in November 1915, he was assigned as transportation officer for the regiment's First Battalion.

Sassoon's poetry of 1914 and early 1915, published in *Discoveries* (1915) and *Morning Glory* (1916), continued in the early Georgian vein, treating war as a gallant quest and a challenge to manhood. The early combat veteran Captain Robert Graves, fellow officer in the First Battalion, Royal Welch Fusiliers, who became Sassoon's good friend and subsequent savior, noted in *Good-bye to All That* that at their first meeting behind the lines, Sassoon "had, at that time, published nothing except a few privately-printed pastoral pieces of eighteen-ninetyish flavour and a satire on Masefield which, about half-way through, had forgotten to be satire and was rather good Masefield."[8] Graves showed Sassoon some of his own war poems, and as he later recalled: "He told me that they were too realistic and that war should not be written about in a realistic way. . . . This was before Siegfried had been in the trenches. I told him, in my old-soldier manner, that he would soon change his style" (Graves, 224). Even the death of his brother Hamo at Gallipoli in August 1915 provoked a poem, "To My Brother," that is depersonalized, and noble death is portrayed as the path to immortality. Later, shocked by the bitterness and brutality of combat on the western front and by the utter misery of the soldiers' troglodyte world, Sassoon would never again write patriotic or limply florid Pre-Raphaelite verse. The Somme scorched it out of him.

Sassoon's actual experience under enemy fire commenced in January 1916 as his battalion took up a position on the river Somme line in preparation for the greatest British-German battle of the war. The Somme offensive, starting on 1 July 1916, cost 420,000 British casualties and nearly as many German. It resulted in minimum British gains, a paltry few miles of captured trenches, but no breakthrough. Now Sassoon knew the disillusionment, the horror, the frustration, and the mind-staggering toll of trench warfare.

Meanwhile Sassoon had developed a close relationship with a handsome young lieutenant named David Thomas, the Dick Tiltwood of *Memoirs of a Fox-hunting Man* (1928), who was shot in the throat and died of the wound on 19 March 1916. Sassoon and Thomas had lived together on leave for a month in 1915 in Cambridge.[9] Sassoon vowed revenge, and every night he went out on voluntary bloodthirsty patrols looking for Germans (Graves, 251).

Sassoon had other close relationships with younger, good-looking officers during the war. The soldier's world was a womanless one, and, of course, there was a great need for affection. Nowhere in Sassoon's poetry or journals of this period is there a favorable mention of a young woman, although deep male friendships are often described. Homosexual activities at the front were, however, almost entirely of the platonic kind, as privacy was rare and the danger of being caught and severely punished extremely grave. Still, for upper-class British officers war was public school all over again. Further, World War I was close in time to the aesthetic movement, with its emphasis on the erotic beauty of young men. Young officers educated at public schools and universities were steeped in a literary tradition of homoeroticism that went back to Greek and Roman roots. Homoerotic motifs were completely natural to them.

In April 1916 Sassoon, still grieving for Thomas, ventured unordered into no-man's-land to bring in wounded comrades. He was awarded the Military Cross for valor. His comrades named him Mad Jack.

The Battle of the Somme was a miserable failure for the British under Field Marshal Douglas "Butcher" Haig. It was four months of hell. A generation of young men was broken. On 6 July 1916 Second Lieutenant Sassoon captured an enemy trench single-handed with Mills bombs (grenades) and was recommended for Britain's highest award for bravery, the Victoria Cross; however, the generals disallowed the award because the overall attack was a failure.

Late in July, as the seemingly unending battle wore on, Lieutenant Sassoon came down with acute gastroenteritis and fever and had to be medically evacuated to England. The illness was lucky, for it most likely saved Sassoon from death or mutilation on the Somme. Recuperating in August 1916 at No. 3 General Hospital, located in Somerville College, Oxford, Sassoon was visited by the art critic Robert (Robbie) Ross, once a friend and lover of Oscar Wilde and now a middle-aged bachelor with many literary and social connections, who had feelings of affections for the young soldier. Ross quickly became Sassoon's enthusiastic patron and impresario. He introduced Sassoon to the notorious and flamboyant artistic doyenne Lady Ottoline Morrell, whose husband was one of the leaders of Britain's small but vocal pacifist movement. Lady Ottoline "collected" Sassoon and invited him to stay for long periods at Garsington, her estate near Oxford.

Soon Sassoon began to undergo a period of radical political education and programmed social climbing. He was introduced by Morrell and Ross to many of the leaders of the cultural and political establishment. Everyone was pleased to meet a genuine romantic war hero who was upper class, handsome, and a poet. Rupert Brooke was dead; Sassoon was alive. During his convalescence leave Sassoon continued to write the aesthetic poetry he had begun on the battlefield, while he comforted his mother—still grieving deeply over the death of Hamo—at Weirleigh.

Meanwhile Ross made the key connection for Sassoon. He took the manuscript of *The Old Huntsman* (1917) to his friend the publisher William Heinemann, who agreed to the publication of a volume of poetry that included several satiric, antiwar poems, the kind Ross had urged Sassoon to produce. It was sure to be controversial. Otherwise friendly and supportive critics like Gosse would later attack it.

Protest

In December 1916 Sassoon was back at the Regimental Depot in Litherfield, near Liverpool, preparing to go out again to France. Waiting for orders "back to the war was in a way more uncomfortable than being out there. The idea of being killed was continually in one's mind. Once one was in the war zone it didn't seem to matter so much and there was no time to worry. I could no longer indulge in fine feelings about being a hero, for although my period of active service had given me confidence in myself as a front-line officer I was ceasing to believe in the war itself."[10] He had, of course, learned of the failure of the Somme offensive, and that his battalion lay in shambles.

On New Year's Eve Sassoon was reading H. G. Wells's antiwar novel *Mr. Britting Sees It Through* (1916). It convinced him finally that the war no longer had any point, that it proceeded from its own mindless momentum (*SJ*, 61). Four months later, back in the line, Sassoon was shot in the shoulder at the Battle of Arras, leading a Mills bomb attack on a German position. Once more he was evacuated to England, where his wound healed quickly in a London hospital. But now, having met with the great pacifist Bertrand Russell, having spoken with Wells and Arnold Bennett, and having received an encouraging letter from his literary idol, Thomas Hardy, whose novels were his constant companions in and out of battle and to whom he dedicated *The Old Huntsman,* Sassoon decided to protest the war in a spectacular Byronic way. He would make what Edmund Blunden called a "splendid war on the war."[11]

On 15 June 1917, having been promised a posting in England, thereby ensuring that his action would not be misconstrued as an attempt to avoid a return to combat, Sassoon wrote his famous *non serviam,* "A Soldier's Declaration":

I am making this statement as an act of wilful defiance of military authority, because I believe that the War is being deliberately prolonged by those who have the power to end it. I am a soldier, convinced that I am acting on behalf of soldiers. I believe that the purposes for which I and my fellow-soldiers entered upon this War should have been so clearly stated as to have made it impossible for them to be changed without our knowledge, and that, had this been done, the objects which actuated us would now be attainable by negotiation.

I have seen and endured the sufferings of the troops, and I can no longer be a party to prolonging those sufferings for ends which I believe to be evil and unjust.

I am not protesting against the military conduct of the War, but against the political errors and insincerities for which the fighting men are being sacrificed.

On behalf of those who are suffering now, I make this protest against the deception which is being practiced on them. Also I believe that it may help to destroy the callous complacence with which the majority of those at home regard the continuance of agonies which they do not share, and which they have not sufficient imagination to realize. (*Diaries 1915–1918,* 173–74)

The protest was sent with a cover letter refusing further military duty to his commanding officer, Commanding Officer of the Third Royal Welch Fusiliers, Litherfield. Copies were sent to influential writers, editors, and politicians, among them Thomas Hardy, Arnold Bennett, H. G. Wells, Edward Marsh, J. A. Spender, Lord Brassey, and Harold Cox. A copy of the protest was printed in the London *Times,* and it was read out in the House of Commons. Sassoon saw his action as the moral equivalent of going over the top. He especially needed to attack the noncombatants on the home front and their "callous complacence" to the terrible agonies "they do not share." Sassoon fully expected a court-martial and martyrdom with concomitant publicity to advance the pacifist cause. It was not to be.

Sassoon's good friend Robert Graves intervened to save him from court-martial, cashiering, and imprisonment for what would probably have been a futile gesture. Graves surreptitiously appealed to Sassoon's senior officers and tried to convince them that his friend was shell-shocked by his combat experiences and that he should be examined by a medical board and be granted indefinite leave to recover. The senior battalion major passed the buck around the absent-on-leave colonel to the commanding general of the Mersey Defenses, who discreetly sent the hot potato on to the War Office, which wisely decided against publicity and for the hushup. The War Office ordered Sassoon before a medical board (Graves, 323–24). Meanwhile, while waiting in Liverpool for the ax to fall, Sassoon went down to the shore at Formby, tore the Military Cross ribbon from his tunic, and threw it into the mouth of the Mersey.

Now Graves had to get to the board before Sassoon. As a fellow officer in the fusiliers he testified that Sassoon had hallucinations, seeing corpses in Piccadilly. Graves fumed: "The irony of having to argue to these mad old men that Siegfried was not sane!" (Graves, 325). Sassoon was sent to a convalescent home for neurasthenics at Craiglockhart, near Edinburgh, where he came under the care of Dr. William H. R. Rivers, a dedicated, intelligent, compassionate psychologist and early Freudian. Their relationship evolved from doctor-patient to that of good friends. Rivers became a father figure for Sassoon. At Craiglockhart Sassoon wrote the poems that would be published in the aptly named *Counter-Attack* (1918), and he befriended and encouraged a young officer patient who was writing poetry. The officer, shaken because his commanding officer had falsely accused him of cowardice, became deeply devoted to the older Sassoon. Graves met and described the young man, Wilfred Owen, as "an idealistic homosexual with a religious background" (Fussell, 289). Sassoon and Owen continued their friendship long after hospitalization ended.

Rivers quickly realized that Sassoon was completely sane. For Sassoon the sham convalescence became untenable. He believed he was betraying his fellow soldiers. Sassoon was a brave man, physically and otherwise, who had felt that only a public protest against war could satisfy his conscience and who had then surrendered to the inevitable when he realized that his superiors were determined to make his protest ineffective by not seriously acknowledging it. With Rivers's reluctant aid, Sassoon managed to pass a medical board examination, be returned to duty status, and manipulate the War Office into sending him out for a third time. Clearly Sassoon was seeking an expiation and vindication through death. On 7 January 1918 he was posted to a battalion in Limerick, Ireland, and then, on 8 February, to the Twenty-fifth Battalion, Royal Welch Fusiliers, in Palestine. With the German breakthrough on the western front early in 1918, Sassoon's battalion was rushed to France in May. Now an acting captain and company commander, Sassoon was able to do more for the men under his command. But on 13 July 1918 Sassoon, returning from a patrol through the long-grass of no-man's-land near Morlancourt, was shot in the head. Ironically, one of his own sergeants had mistaken him for a German. The path home was familiar: dressing station, field hospital, embarkation port, and general hospital in England, this time the American Women's Hospital in Lancaster Gate, London. Now he was one of Britain's most famous battle casualties. And with the publication of *Counter-Attack* Siegfried Sassoon's reputation as one of Britain's premier war poets was firmly and permanently established.

Armistice

Released from the hospital, Sassoon continued his recovery at Lennel House, near Coldstream in Berwickshire, and then at Weirleigh. Early in October 1918 Arnold Bennett, then deputy minister at the Ministry of Information, tried to obtain a post for Sassoon on the staff of Lord Beaverbrook, the minister, to prevent his shipping out again for France. Sassoon received a letter offering him a post and asking for his qualifications. Surprised and disinclined, Sassoon replied that his only qualification for a job in the Ministry of Information was that he had been wounded in the head (*SJ*, 106).

On 3 October Sassoon was summoned to London by Edward Marsh, who had been working as private secretary to Winston Churchill, then minister of munitions. Marsh too wanted to keep Sassoon from risking his life again and, knowing that Churchill had admired Sassoon's poetry, hoped to obtain for his protégé a position in the ministry. It was a grotesque absurdity for Sassoon that he should be considered for such a posting, but out of politeness toward Marsh and interest in Churchill, the pacifist-soldier attended the interview. The conversation quickly became a Churchillian, cigar-in-the-mouth monologue on the glorious achievements of mechanized warfare, concluding with Churchill declaring, "War is the normal occupation of man . . . war and gardening" (*SJ*, 119).

At the beginning of November 1918 Marsh introduced Sassoon to a "somewhat distinguished Colonel" (*SJ*, 128), just back from Arabia. It was T. E. Lawrence, and they would be friends for the remainder of Lawrence's troubled life. On 7 November 1918, only four days before the unexpected armistice, Sassoon finally met his literary idol, the author whose works he had devoured before, during, and after battles in France, Egypt, and Palestine: Thomas Hardy. The Grand Old Man of English letters invited Sassoon to Max Gate. Sassoon remained devoted to Hardy until the novelist's death in 1928. Sassoon also received an invitation to visit the future poet laureate John Masefield, who then took the younger poet to meet the present laureate, Robert Bridges.

Meanwhile, on 4 November 1918, only a week before the armistice and after winning the Military Cross, Wilfred Owen, only 25 years old, was machine-gunned to death on the Sambre Canal. The telegram arrived at his parents' home in Shrewsbury one hour after the armistice bells began to ring at 11:00 A.M. on 11 November. The news was kept from Sassoon. Months later, when he was informed, he grieved deeply for his lost friend. He went to Owen's mother and obtained his poems, only four of which had been published. Sassoon arranged for an edition of Owen's poetry to be published in 1920, and thus founded the reputation of the other great World War I poet. Sassoon's generous action was a great gift to English poetry.

Even though he knew nothing of Owen's death, the armistice gave Sassoon no joy. Like many combat veterans, he was depressed. The war had cost more than 700,000 British lives. Yet Captain Sassoon had triumphed over war. Interestingly, he would be called Captain Sassoon all the rest of his life, especially by the villagers of Heyetesbury, where he later established his home. He did not object to the warrior title, perhaps because he wanted people to remember which Sassoon he was and how he had stood up for his principles. Yet some thought the title odd for a pacifist. Others, such as Wilfred Owen's brother, the artist Harold Owen, whom Sassoon befriended and helped, noted the seemingly irreconcilable aspects of his character: his compassionate poetry, his fierce killing of Germans even though he was against the war, and his lust to hunt and slay the fox.[12] In retrospect Sassoon seems unlike the traditional, fully committed pacifists such as the Quakers. Rather, he was against wars for imperialistic or economic reasons wherein youth were deluded, lied to, and sacrificed in the name of patriotism. In World War II Sassoon was not a pacifist. Fascism had to be destroyed in order to save Western civilization.

Postwar

Captain Sassoon was not officially retired for wounds until 12 March 1919. *Picture-Show* was issued in June and *The War Poems of Siegfried Sassoon* in October, both to great acclaim. Sassoon now considered himself a political radical, and thus he enrolled in an economics curriculum at Oxford in order to help the Labour party; he soon grew bored with the Dismal Science, however, and quit.

Meanwhile a rushed general election was called by Prime Minister David Lloyd George. This event was termed the Khaki Election because so many soldiers were still in uniform and mostly unable to vote. Sassoon was asked to campaign for a Pacifist Socialist parliamentary candidate. To do so meant an open break with the politics and values of his family. Sensitized by the sufferings of the enlisted soldiers in the war, Sassoon agreed to campaign despite his diffidence as an orator and his shyness that made it hard for him even in his thirties to look people in the eye as he spoke. He campaigned for the Pacifist Socialist Philip Snowden, running for the seat from Blackburn in the industrial North, not exactly a fox-hunter's home territory. Snowden lost but was later vindicated by achieving high office in future governments. Sassoon quit formal politics but continued to support Labour.

Sassoon worked hard at literary networking. John and Ada Galsworthy took him under their wings. Walter de la Mare, Wilfred Gibson, John Middleton Murry, and Virginia Woolf, who reviewed *Counter-*

Attack in the *Times Literary Supplement,* became friends. George Bernard Shaw; Edith, Osbert, and Sacheverell Sitwell; and Hilaire Belloc joined his circle. Max Beerbohm, whom he had met in 1916 at the Gosses', grew closer even though Beerbohm returned to Italy. Max and Siegfried became lifelong friends. *War Poems* (1919) confirmed literary stardom. At this time Sassoon, to his own surprise, accepted a paying job. A new newspaper, the socialist *Daily Herald,* "The Paper with Its Face towards the Future," asked him to be its first literary editor at a salary of £5 a week (*SJ,* 204–6). Sassoon's Conservative mother referred to his newspaper as "that rabid and pestulent rag" (*SJ,* 212).

At the *Daily Herald* Sassoon went to work in a bright red tie and published satiric pieces from a socialist viewpoint. But his satires were uneasy and awkward because the issues of the time were not as clear-cut to him as were those in the war. Moreover, the fervor, passion, and intensity of his wartime poetry began to diminish rapidly. He had made war on war; now there was no such target for his anger, and neither was there an object for his affection. The newspaper assignment did not last, and the most significant result of editorship for Sassoon was his discovery of the young war poet Edmund Blunden, another lifelong friend.

Sassoon spent almost all of 1920 in North America on a lecture-and-poetry-reading tour, where he was feted as a Byronic hero. He met many leading American poets, including Edwin Markham, Edwin Arlington Robinson, Amy Lowell, and a young Edna St. Vincent Millay. Carl Sandburg took him on a tour of Chicago, and the playwright S. N. Behrman showed him New York. Sassoon was not a great hit on the platform, but admirers forgave him. One woman came up to the stage after a reading to tell him how much his "magnetic silences" had meant to her (*SJ,* 269). Others did not take kindly to his antiwar message.

Sassoon returned to England to take up residence in London at 54 Tufton Street and later 23 Campden Hill Square. In October 1931 he rented Fitz House, Teffont Magna, Wiltshire, where, having grown reclusive and desiring country life again, he resided until his marriage in 1933. But in 1921 he was still dreaming of battle.[13] *Recreations* (1923), a collection of satiric poems, shows Sassoon struggling for subject matter. Sassoon's sexual interest at this time was homosexual (*Diaries 1920–1922,* 205–87 passim). His vacillating attitude toward his own sexuality troubled him throughout most of his life. Now young artistic and aristocratic men 20 years his junior became his lovers and live-in companions, particularly the artist Stephen Tennant, later in the decade.[14]

Sassoon's lovers were always effeminate younger men and his role in the relationships was not the passive, receptive part, so his sexual choices did not mar his gender self-image of a country gentleman and ex-soldier.

Trips abroad to Italy to visit Max Beerbohm in Rapallo, and to France and Germany; an epicurean life in the exciting world of literature and art; and public recognition provided less and less happiness for Sassoon. The war had left him an enigmatic, nervous man, lost in a lost generation, and without God. Death had chosen favorites, and he had not been one. Rejected, he spent a lifetime longing for the lost battalions. Slowly and only eventually he would try to bring himself back to religion and find purpose in the last half of his life (Corrigan, 39).

Rewriting Life

The publication of Sassoon's *Selected Poems* (1925) was the high water mark of his reputation as a poet, but most of the poems had already been published in earlier volumes. *Satirical Poems* (1926) reprinted his later pieces from the more recent collections, and readers could readily see the falling-off in passion and purpose. Technique once more overcame topic. Yet Sassoon's main literary activity for the next 20 years was the rewriting of his life to his thirty-fourth year. Thus he created for himself a second and then a third youth, growing old but living in a sometimes happier, sometimes tragic, but always more intense past.

First Sassoon selected, highlighted, and slightly fictionalized the countryman aspect of his early life. *Memoirs of a Fox-hunting Man* (1928) introduced Sassoon's alter ego, George Sherston, to a delighted literary world. The fictionalized autobiography received two of Britain's highest awards for fiction, the Hawthornden Prize and the James Tait Black Memorial Prize. Its success encouraged Sassoon to continue in the autobiographical vein. *Memoirs of an Infantry Officer* (1930) stands as one of the great World War I combat memoirs, along with those of his friends: Edmund Blunden's *Undertones of War* (1928) and Robert Graves's *Goodbye to All That* (1929). *Sherston's Progress* (1936) completed the portrait of a parsed Sassoon. The memoirs were republished in a single volume in 1937 as *The Complete Memoirs of George Sherston*. Then Sassoon started all over again, this time writing his life as pure autobiography with *The Old Century and Seven More Years* (1938), reputedly Sassoon's favorite book (Corrigan, 33), which tells of his life through 1907; *The Weald of Youth* (1942), autobiography to 1914; and *Siegfried's Journey 1916–1920* (1945). Sassoon continued to write and publish poetry during the long run of autobiographical writing. *The Heart's Journey* (1927), *Vigils* (1934), and *Rhymed Ruminations* (1939) are meditative collections centered on a search for "selfhood's essence," or the human soul. They also contain nostalgic and sentimental descriptive poems of environs, home, and family. The poems in *Road to Ruin* (1933) are political pieces warning against the resurgence of European militarism.

In 1931 Sassoon received the honorary Doctor of Letters (D.Litt.) degree from Liverpool University. He was then very much a part of the literary establishment, but poetry critics began to pay less attention to him. The 1930s through the 1950s saw a slow but steady decline in reader interest in Sassoon, while he took less and less interest in the changing climate and fashions of verse, until by the late 1950s he was virtually ignored. Sassoon had found the work of modernists like Ezra Pound and T. S. Eliot and imagists like Amy Lowell to be uncongenial; the Thirties Poets—W. H. Auden, Stephen Spender, Louis MacNeice, and C. Day Lewis—seemed politically and aesthetically wrongheaded, writing propaganda instead of poetry; and superstylists like Dylan Thomas were in the fireworks business. Sassoon, no longer a realist, satiric poet with an agenda, reverted to Georgianism and religious verse. Another strong reason for Sassoon's retreat to memories of youth and the poetry of the past was the rise of national socialism. The Nuremberg racial laws deeply disturbed this man of ancient Jewish ancestry, who realized before most that yet another day of death was dawning over Europe and he was helpless to do anything about it.

Marriage

Although Sassoon seemed never to have solved the doubts of sexuality, he did marry. Rejected and abandoned by his lover Stephen Tennant after a long and passionate relationship, Sassoon on 18 December 1933 wedded Hester Gatty, daughter of the late chief justice of Gibraltar, Sir Stephen Herbert Gatty. Sassoon had first seen Hester at the Wilton Pageant on 9 June 1933. They were introduced in September and became engaged after a whirlwind courtship. Hester was 28; Siegfried, 47. At their small, quiet wedding in Christchurch the guests included T. E. Lawrence. They cruised to Spain, Sicily, and mainland Italy for their honeymoon and then made their home at Heytesbury House, Heytesbury, Wiltshire, where Sassoon would live out his life. The marriage produced one child, a son, George, born in 1936. The marriage was not successful. The couple drifted apart and separated after 10 years, although they never divorced. A friendship lingered, and Hester even helped nurse Sassoon when illness struck him in his last years. Sassoon and George remained close throughout the father's lifetime. George became an electronics engineer and undertook research at Cambridge. Hester died in 1973.

World War II

Sassoon was not opposed to British entry into World War II. Early on he realized that fascism had to be stopped and that force was the only way to do it. He opened Heytesbury House to war refugees in 1940, an example of the many quiet acts of charity Sassoon performed in his mature years. In 1942 a company of King's Royal Rifles, with 20 Bren gun carriers, was bivouacked at Heytesbury House, and on the adjoining grounds, the beautiful estate park, 200 military vehicles were parked. A brigadier general and a brigade staff were quartered in Sassoon's dining room. Soldiers were snoring everywhere. The next year the British troops were replaced by Americans, and the park of Heytesbury House was turned into a regimental camp for 1,500 Yanks, Nissen huts, and full equipment (Corrigan, 34). Long before, Sassoon had retreated to a bedroom and a study, reading and working through the night, and sleeping as best he could through the din of the day. If the old soldier could not go to war, the war surely came to him. Not surprisingly Sassoon published no new poetry during World War II.

Postwar Once More

Sassoon employed some of his time after the war to culminating his long, admiring interest in George Meredith by writing the biography *Meredith* (1948). After Faber published *Collected Poems* in 1947, most of Sassoon's new poetry was published privately in limited editions: *Common Chords* (1950), *Emblems of Experience* (1951), and *The Tasking* (1954). The subjects include nature and religion, remembrances of days past and people gone, descriptions of dreams, and the joy of solitude. Incorporating 62 poems from these books into one volume, Faber published *Sequences* in 1956.

Twenty-nine religious poems from the earlier post–World War II collections were published in *The Path to Peace* (1960). The vein of poetry had just about run out, but Sassoon was a healthy septuagenarian. He still played a good, competitive game of cricket. He lived simply and ate little, keeping the lean body profile of youth. He spent as much time in outdoor activities as was feasible.

Taps

Sassoon's last years brought him several honors. In 1951 he was made a Commander, Order of the British Empire. Two years later his old college at Cambridge, Clare, which he had left sans degree, made him an Honorary Fellow. Queen Elizabeth II awarded him the Gold Medal in poetry in 1957. In 1965 Oxford conferred on him an honorary Doctor of Letters.

Sassoon's increasing soul-searching and God-seeking led him finally to conversion to Roman Catholicism. For a long time he had sought and enjoyed conversation and discourse with Catholic clergy. He was received into the church on 14 August 1957 in Downside Church. Catholicism brought great peace to Sassoon at age 70.

In 1961 *Collected Poems 1908–1956* was published by Faber. It is Sassoon's monument. The book marks his place in British poetry. A final publication, *An Octave* (1966), presents eight poems of serenity and quiet faith. It was privately published to commemorate Sassoon's eightieth birthday, preceding his death by a few months.

There was one last soldier's victory for Sassoon. Loyal to Edmund Blunden to the end but estranged from Graves, Sassoon helped the former to buy a cottage in Long Melford, Suffolk, advancing some of the money he intended to leave Blunden in his will (Jackson, 291). In 1966 Sassoon aided in the successful campaign to elect Blunden to the prestigious Oxford Professorship of Poetry over the American Robert Lowell. Blunden died in 1974; Graves, in 1985.

Siegfried Sassoon, the countryman, came to the end of his days peacefully, dying in his sleep at Heytesbury House on 1 September 1967 in the presence of his son. He was buried in Mells churchyard, Somerset. His long spiritual quest had ended, or perhaps had just begun.

Chapter Two

"Young Nimrod"

Early Poems

While a student at Clare College, Cambridge, the neophyte poet Siegfried Sassoon tried on Tennyson's hat and cloak (Lane, 87). That act is symbolic of the fact that Sassoon's pre–World War I poetry, and even some of his postwar poetry, is deeply rooted in the nineteenth century. The early poetry evinces little of the shock, power, corrosiveness, and vitality of the 1916–18 combat poems, because his early efforts were the work of a complacent, dilettante, privileged young man of his time, one as much in love with fox-hunting, horses, golf, and cricket as he was with poetry.

Yet poetry filled a primal need in Sassoon to express his love of the natural world, to provide a vent for his sensitive feelings, to create as he consumed, to communicate self in a social milieu devoted to superficial congress and stilted oral and written expression, and to become part of the greater world of arts and letters that his association with his Thornycroft relatives and his sojourn at Cambridge had opened to him. Poetry could also give meaning and purpose to a life that otherwise would be unremembered and unrecorded. Thus the frivolous playboy, unbeknownst to most of his sporting friends, many of whom would have been shocked, doubtful, derisive, and disdainful of the knowledge, published 14 small volumes of poetry between 1906 and 1916. Thirteen of them were privately published at Sassoon's expense, and only one, *The Redeemer* (1916), a single poem reprinted from the *Cambridge Magazine,* was a commercial publication.

Sassoon's early poems are always derivative, and frequently stilted, self-conscious, pallid, and strained. The diction is Victorian or earlier. The style is Pre-Raphaelite with the residue of exposure to the aesthetic movement and the Celtic Twilight, although Sassoon never mentions Yeats in describing his background and reading in poetry. Like the Pre-Raphaelites and decadents of his reading, Sassoon rejected the contemporary industrialized world outside his beloved Kentish Weald. Sassoon apparently knew nothing of Mallarmé and French symbolism. Thus Sassoon, although writing poetry into the Edwardian era, did not engage in the Edwardian political and artistic liberalization or in the attack on the philosophical and aesthetic values of the fin de siècle years.[1] What Sassoon did accomplish in his early verse was a competence in versification and a sharpening of his observing eye.

First Publications

Sassoon had a long and leisurely apprenticeship. The series of privately printed pamphlets, 10 to 50 copies in an edition, to be distributed to relatives and friends, commenced with *Poems* (1906), a collection of 22 pieces, and was followed by a one-act verse play, *Orpheus in Diloeryum* (1908); *Sonnets and Verses* (1909), 34 poems; *Sonnets* (1909), 17 poems, 11 of which were from *Sonnets and Verses; Twelve Sonnets* (1911), only 2 of which were new; *Poems* (1911), 12 poems; *Hyacinth: An Idyll,* a prose play about love, incorporating 6 pieces of verse; *An Ode for Music* (1912), 6 stanzas; *Discoveries* (1915), 13 poems; and *Morning-Glory* (1916), 11 poems. Two additional publications were meant for a wider readership and were published commercially: *The Daffodil Murderer* (1913), by "Saul Kain" (1,000 copies printed), intended as a parody of John Masefield's extremely popular *The Everlasting Mercy* (1911), and *The Redeemer* (1916; 200–250 copies printed).[2] *Orpheus in Diloeryum* was printed in an edition of only 5 copies on handmade paper. Dissatisfied with the text, Sassoon revised it but refused to pay a second £10 for printer's corrections, and so the second edition was aborted. Apparently no copy of the revision exists. Sassoon was so unhappy with a second look at his work in *Sonnets and Verses* when it arrived from the printer that he burned all but 4 copies (*WY*, 25).

Self-Criticism

The mature Sassoon was justly hard on his early work: "Worse lyrics have probably been written at two-and-twenty. But the question—what exactly *should* I sing—was one which so far I had not asked myself with any awareness of the circumstance that, like many minstrels of my age, I had nothing much to sing about" (*WY*, 24). Young Sassoon thought that poetry came out of "a distillation of imagination which was strangely and exquisitely remote from everyday experience. The result was that pseudo-archaic precosities invaded my vocabulary. Sunsets became like stained-glass windows, and the moon took to coming up in a mystification of Celtic twilight. Poetry was a dream world into which I escaped through an esoteric door in my mind" (*WY,* 28). No aesthete can ever be psychologically prepared for the horrors of modern war. Sassoon's early poetry prepared him technically as a poet. His youth prepared him for anything but battle. In this juxtaposition lies the essence of his art.

Sonnets and Verses

Sassoon chose only 29 poems from his 1906–16 efforts as worthy of preserving, somewhat revised, in *Collected Poems 1908–1956* (1961). Additionally, "By the Way" is included in *The Weald of Youth* (*WY,* 23–24) and *The Daffodil Murderer* is available in Michael Thorpe's *Siegfried Sassoon: A Critical Study*[3] and elsewhere. "Villon," "October," "Morning-Land," "Arcady Unheeding," and "By the Way" from *Sonnets and Verses* are the earliest. "Villon," a Petrarchan sonnet in Swinburnian fashion, describes the French medieval poet as thrown from the gates of Paris, "my matted hair / Was dank with dungeon wetness; my spent frame / O'erlaid with marish argues." The poor man, unlike the affluent author, knew what it was to be "tortured by leaping pangs of frost and flame."[4]

The sonnet "October" shows Sassoon intoxicated with the medieval archaisms of Dante Gabriel Rossetti: lots of "ye"s, slopes are "flower-kirtled," and "the drooping cherry orchards of October / Like mournful pennons hang their shrivelling leaves / Russet and orange" (*CP 1908–1956,* 52). "Morning-Land" praises "Old English songs," while "Arcady Unheeding" finds "Shepherds whistling on their way" (*CP 1908–1956,* 55). But it is up to "By the Way" to summarize young Sassoon's poetic difficulties: "Touching his lute by the way, / What shall the minstrel sing?" (*WY,* 23).

Sonnets and Twelve Sonnets

The final version of "Before Day" is set in Arcady again, and the singer enigmatically laments, "I am alone, a dweller among men / Hungered for what my heart shall never say" (*CP 1908–1956,* 64). The poem has a Keatsian richness, however, if also an adolescent melancholy and a sense of imminent loss of innocence. "Goblin Revel," from *Twelve Sonnets,* moves like a *danse macabre,* evoking medieval times with jangling dulcimers and "shoon," dialect for shoes, making no noise.

Poems

Poems (1911) is represented in *Collected Poems 1908–1956* by "An Old French Poet," "Dryads," and "At Daybreak." The first is one of several early poems in which Death personified concludes both life and the poem in a maudlin, melancholy way, not atypical in youthful verse. The persona's dead voice sends "A fading message from the misty shores of dream" (*CP 1908–1956,* 53). In this rhetorical manner Sassoon indicates an early interest in communication between the dead and the living, a subject that will engage him more fully after World War I.

"Dryads" is representative of Sassoon's early, affected pastoralism. He is writing about wood nymphs in the Edwardian world of arms races and rampant imperialism. The poem is hardly more than an exercise in singsong verbiage:

> The cocks that crow to the land
>   Are faint and hollow and shrill:
> Dryads brown as the leaf
>   Whisper, and hide, and are still.
>
> (CP 1908–1956, 54)

The homoerotic "At Daybreak" presents the persona waiting for a male lover, who is the "Spirit of purity." The memory of the lover's "fair, unshadowed face" abides with the persona "until tomorrow." The 12-line poem has a charm that is marred only by language like "Loth was he ever to forsake me" (*CP 1908–1956,* 55).

Melodies

The Petrarchan sonnets "Night-Piece" and "The Heritage" represent *Melodies* in *Collected Poems 1908–1956.* Dryads appear again in the former, while "baleful shapes . . . moan" in Pre-Raphaelite lush (*CP 1908–1956,* 51). Death is "The Heritage," but "within his very presence yet we dare / To gather gladness like a fading flower" (*CP 1908–1956,* 53). These poems are fairly indicative of young Sassoon's inability to recognize and either modify or reject outmoded poetic forms and techniques.

Discoveries

Sassoon chose 10 poems from *Discoveries* for saving and inclusion in *Collected Poems 1908–1956.* Some of these pieces mark a transition from apprenticeship to journeyman status. Still with singsong regularity "Nimrod in September" "makes / Huge clamour in the sultry brakes" (*CP 1908–1956*, 44), and "Noah" when "Earth was saved ... danced a jig" (*CP 1908–1956*, 46). "To-day" is personification-ridden with "Night who stilled / The ghost of Yester-eve" and "fair Morn / The mother of To-morrow" (*CP 1908–1956*, 57). "Wonderment" is obscure in its nature worship by "The wise / Who gaze breathing wonderment" (*CP 19089–1956*, 58), and "Daybreak in a Garden" has "farm cocks crowing," of course, and "nodding peony-flowers" (*CP 1908–1956*, 59). "Companions" are the birds with their "slender bird-song sweet." A "gentle breeze" and a "golden cloud" are among the cloying clichés in this poem of four pedestrian couples (*CP 1908–1956*, 59).

"Southwind," however, shows Sassoon beginning to break away from singsong and doggerel, and twisted language. He is able to address the rough wind simply: "I forgave you / When you stole to me shyly with scent of hawthorn," simultaneously encoding a personal love lyric (*CP 1908–1956*, 60). Figures come to life, metaphors work better, and clichés diminish. "Tree and Sky" shocks the contemporary reader knowing Sassoon's later life, as the persona prays to the "tempests in / My spirit, let them surge like din / Of noble melodies at war," and there is mention of flashing blades and "shafts of glory" (*CP 1908–1956*, 61). Sassoon used battle metaphor in a romantic, plausive manner even as a soldier, but only until the first experience of actual combat.

The three-quatrain poem "Alone" evinces cognitive questioning and deeper thoughts, with the persona wondering why "in my sense survives / Only the impulse of those lives / That were my making" (*CP 1908–1956*, 61). And "Wisdom" well expresses his satisfaction, perhaps even smugness, with his life and work to that time: "I look within me to the edge of dark, / and dream, 'The world's my field, and I'm the lark'" (*CP 1908–1956*, 64).

Clearly Sassoon was also satisfied with his development as a poet. *Discoveries* was not repudiated like most of and much in the earlier collections. Almost all of *Discoveries* was included in *The Old Huntsman* (1917), Sassoon's first significant book of poetry.

Morning-Glory

All 11 poems of *Morning-Glory* are reprinted in *The Old Huntsman*, and all 11 appear in *Collected Poems 1908–1956*. Although Sassoon had not yet found his realistic and satiric voice, his apprenticeship was long over and his journeymanship nearly concluded too. The poems in *Morning-Glory* indicate further artistic progress and developing ratiocinative power. The poem "Ancestors" even finds Sassoon evincing some interest in his Sephardic Jewish ancestry and its ancient relations with caliphs, sultans, and shahs. He projects and experiences that interest in the florid, sensuous language of Masefield's "Cargoes" (1902). The poem is an archetypal dream of and from the past. A gallery of jeweled, turbaned ancestors gather, trade, and sometimes sing their prayers. Then:

> A silent-footed message flits and brings
> The ghostly Sultan from his glimmering halls;
> A shadow at the window, turbaned, vast,
> He leans; and, pondering the sweet influence
> That steals around him in remembered flowers,
> Hears the frail music wind along the slopes,
> Put forth, and fade across the whispering sea.
>
> *(CP 1908–1956,* 47)

"Ancestors" is more evocative than any other early vintage Sassoon poem. He has moved from personalized trivialization to objectivism and has become a poet of his time. With its escapist cosmopolitanism and sensuality, "Ancestors" is pure Georgian.

With "Blind" Sassoon is abandoning subjectivism. He is moving out of himself and finding themes beyond his immediate experience. Here he shows compassion for others instead of weltschmerz and self-pity. Again an image in early Sassoon seems to prophesy terrible "sights" yet to come into focus. The blind man, whose "thoughts that once in eager strife / Leapt sure from eye to brain and back to eye" (*CP 1908–1956,* 49), reminds us of images of World War I soldiers, blinded by poison gas, groping their way "With feeble steps and fingers on the wall" (*CP 1908–1956,* 49).

"Dream-Forest," however, reverts to inverted archaic language, but "A Child's Prayer," like the title sonnet, "Morning-Glory," is an early religious poem of Sassoon's. In it he asks Jesus to "guard my innocence forevermore" (*CP 1908–1956,* 57). The theme of religion will dominate Sassoon's last poetry.

"A Poplar and the Man" and "Wind in the Beechwood" are typical, early Sassoon nature poems, the latter a sonnet in which the poet exhibits a dreamy but convincing pantheism:

> [L]et me fade
> In the warm, rustling music of the hours
> That guard your ancient wisdom, till my dream
> Moves with the chant and whisper of the glade.
>
> (*CP 1908–1956,* 63)

In *Collected Poems* (1947) and *Collected Poems 1908–1956* Sassoon chose to place four 1914–15 poems from *Morning-Glory* in the section entitled "War Poems: 1915–1917" instead of in "Lyrical Poems: 1908–1916," where the other *Morning-Glory* poems are situated. They are indeed "war poems," but they are precombat efforts, in a sense civilian poems on war themes, contrasting sharply with the bitterly ironic poems in *Counter-Attack* (1918) and *Picture-Show* (1919).

"To My Brother," called "Brother" in *Morning-Glory,* is a poignant piece. Hamo Sassoon was killed at Gallipoli in 1915, and Sassoon and his family suffered great anguish over the untimely death of the youngest. But the patriotic poet, under the influence of Rupert Brooke's "The Dead" (1914), was still caught up in jingoism and the strange ecstasy infecting Europeans early in the war. Sassoon sees through "the gloom," his brother's "laurell'd head / And through your victory I shall win the light" (*CP 1908–1956,* 12). The Battle of the Somme would soon show that there was no "light" to be won.

"The Dragon and the Undying" also romanticizes war. The dead are not mutilated, butchered corpses. Rather, "Their faces are the fair, unshrouded night, / And planets are their eyes" (*CP 1908–1956,* 12). In "To Victory" the persona's attitude toward war shifts slightly. Victory does not bring revenge or retribution or blood satisfaction. What the poet hopes for is a return to the prewar status quo with "colours that were my joy / Not in the woeful crimson of men slain, / But shining as a garden," for he is "tired of the greys and browns and the leafless ash." Not yet having heard it, however, he can only describe massive artillery fire as "the angry guns that boom and flash" (*CP 1908–1956,* 13).

"To His Dead Body" laments the death of Robert Graves, mistakenly reported killed in action. The poem "describes" the death in sanitized, conventional terms. The soldier's death is painless, as it seldom is in battle. The soul transcends mortality, climbing to "gleaming fields to find new day," where the soldier will see "Dear, red-faced Father God who lit your mind" (*CP 1908–1956,* 22).

The Daffodil Murderer

Sassoon did not include *The Daffodil Murderer* in his two *Collected Poems,* because it began as a parody of John Masefield's *The Everlasting Mercy* and was published under the pseudonym Saul Kain, like Masefield's tavern-brawling protagonist Saul Kane. In addition, friends and some critics thought more of the long narrative than Sassoon did. The title derives from Masefield's narrative *The Daffodil Fields* (1913), published as Sassoon was writing his parody. *The Daffodil Murderer* is "Sassoon's most promising pre-War poem" (Thorpe, 9). The text is available in Thorpe's *Siegfried Sassoon: A Critical Study* (Thorpe, 273–86). The poem is Sassoon's longest, at 557 lines in rhymed couplets.

Although *The Daffodil Murderer* begins as a burlesque of Masefield, the poem develops a human appeal of its own. Sassoon found himself carried away "not only with abundant delight but a descriptive energy quite unlike anything I had experienced before" (*WY,* 117). After some 50 lines the poet was intensely trapped in the work and the character of the Sussex farmer awaiting trial for the accidental murder of the barman of a village alehouse. Sassoon brings person and place to life. John Masefield, later Sassoon's friend, had unknowingly helped him to find "a new pair of poetic legs" (*WY,* 119). Sassoon switched from admiring parodist to rivaling narrator, and his work was praised by Edmund Gosse and Edward Marsh. Most significantly, in Sassoon's words "it was the first sign of my being capable of writing as I did during the war, and the first time I used real experience" (Corrigan, 68).

Masefield's *The Everlasting Mercy* is a product of "English evangelical revivalism."[5] In it a brutish, wastrel poacher reforms and turns revivalist when converted and saved by a Quaker woman. Sassoon's Saul Kain is a Sussex farm laborer who drinks. When he accidentally kills a barman and is condemned to death, he dictates his story to the prison chaplain. Unlike Masefield's Saul, he has not undergone a religious experience. He is not saved. He longs only for peace when he is "away and out beyond" (Thorpe, 285; l. 516).

The Daffodil Murderer is at its best when simplest and unaffected:

> There's one I'd like to have a word with,
> And get a hand-shake to be cheer'd with;

And tell 'im I took no offence
For how he treated me long since.

(Thorpe, 284; ll. 500–503)

Sassoon is beginning to use the natural Wordsworthian language
he would later advocate in *On Poetry* (1939). He is unknowingly prepar-
ing for verisimilitudinous dialogue and description in war. Moreover,
Sassoon has come to perhaps an unconscious realization that local
farmhands and their dialect were more familiar and authentic than the
ghosts and goblins he had been writing about. "The Old Huntsman"
(1917), with its lifelike central character in the Masefield mode, "is be-
ginning to take shape."[6] Sassoon is striving for what will be the salient
characteristic of his wartime poetry: authenticity.

The Daffodil Murderer does have some power to move the reader to
feeling pain and sympathizing with the protagonist. Sassoon's technical
ability to evoke, to re-create, is growing. *The Daffodil Murderer* sounds
tin-eared, however, when the country dialect does not work, the dis-
course is pedestrian or even banal, and the rhymes are strained: "Ted
never had the guts to do it; / I done the job and got to rue it" (Thorpe,
283; ll. 460–61).

Although *The Daffodil Murderer* is a journeyman piece, it shows the
promise of the Sassoon yet to come, when true misery on a vast scale de-
manded chronicling and poetic treatment. The friendly critics, such as
Gosse and Marsh, were correct in taking notice.

Sassoon's Pastoralism

Sassoon's early poetry evokes a reclusive countryman's vision of a pas-
toral dream world, one in which a budding poet writes more from the
experience of his reading than from that of his life. Clearly he loved the
Kentish countryside, and that love moved him to artistic expression.
Further, Sassoon possessed a competitive drive to do things well, and
although he hid the fact, he worked as hard on his poetry as he did on
his golf game. He did not write about heterosexual love as lyric poets
conventionally do, but that was not his orientation. His forms and
techniques were conservative. He was, then, basically a Georgian roman-
tic, though he owed much to the Pre-Raphaelites and the Rhymers'
Club. He looked to Algernon Swinburne, Dante Gabriel Rossetti,
Ernest Dowson, George Meredith, John Masefield, and eventually
Thomas Hardy for models.

Sassoon first thought that pseudomedieval language, subjects, and situations meant poetry. Additionally, it must be remembered that Sassoon came from a family of artists and musicians. They worked with color and sound. As one critic has pointed out, "When, therefore, at a very early age, [Sassoon] took to making art objects out of words, he handled them as his family handled pigments and marble chords. Words were things, to be arranged so as to convey sensations, and to evoke feelings."[7] (In fact that is how most romantic poetry operates.)

After the long apprenticeship and journeymanship an authentic, original, and significant poetic voice was about to emerge. That voice was realistic, satiric, and prophetic. In this regard Masefield was the master from whom Sassoon took lessons. In the older poet and in that distinct part of the Georgian poetic which "contained realistic tendencies that culminated in the directness, brutality, and honesty of his best war verses,"[8] Sassoon located a political discourse that would serve him well.

Chapter Three
"Golgotha"
World War I Poems

From a literary critic's viewpoint, one of the outstanding aspects of World War I is the amount of excellent poetry it inspired. What is perhaps the greatest body of war poetry ever written was produced by British poets from 1914 to 1918. Indeed those few bloody years spawned two "generations" of war poets: the first caught up in the awful and blind patriotism of the hour, among them Rupert Brooke, Julian Grenfell, Robert Nichols, Charles Sorley, and the pre-Somme Sassoon, and the second "composed of" antiwar satirists and soldier-poets of pity and disillusionment, among them Sassoon, Wilfred Owen, Isaac Rosenberg, Robert Graves, and Edmund Blunden.

Bernard Bergonzi, in *Heroes' Twilight: A Study of the Literature of the Great War,* notes that the prewar Sassoon "typified an *echt*-Georgian state of mind. Whatever radicalism he manifested during the war was forced upon him by events."[1] Self-trained by years of writing poetry, Sassoon had developed a good ear and eye for detail. Most of all he knew that

the writing of poetry was a serious matter to be undertaken carefully, deliberately. It was not to be achieved, as it was with so many of the amateurs, merely by allowing powerful emotions to overflow spontaneously on to a piece of paper in whatever ragged form happened to come most readily to hand. Even in the midst of trench warfare Sassoon labored over his poems, corrected, inserted, emended, to bring them to as near perfection as he was able; he constantly made notes of the scenes he saw and the emotions he experienced so that the poems he would write from them later might have the ring of authenticity; he carefully stored to overflowing both his memory and his notebooks.[2]

Additionally, Sassoon had absorbed an important lesson in language. From Masefield he had learned to listen carefully to conversation and to write in everyday language. What his eyes saw and his ears heard, his brain absorbed and his hand wrote. As Bernard Bergonzi explains, "Sassoon was forced by the need for exactness in registering front-line experience into a degree of colloquial language and a conversational tone that was still a novelty in contemporary verse" (Bergonzi, 102). The language of modern war thus entered English poetry.

Of course, those who looked back to Victorian poetry for models and standards, and the early modernists like Yeats, Pound, and Eliot, did not consider verisimilar dialogue to be the workings of "real" poetry. John Middleton Murry, the young advocate of modernism, in reviewing Sassoon's best-selling *Counter-Attack* in the 13 July 1918 issue of the *Nation,* decided that Sassoon's work was "not poetry." Sassoon was merely in torment and crying aloud, and by inference "his cry is incoherent." Sassoon's existence, presumably as a fire-eating antiwar activist, is important, "not the poetry." For the objectivist Murry "True art . . . is the evidence of a man's triumph over his experience." Sassoon's language, on the other hand, is "overwrought, dense and turgid." Most damning is the comment that "the unforgettable horror of an inhuman experience can only be rightly rendered by rendering also its relation to the harmony and calm which it shatters. . . . The quality of an experience can only be given by reference to the ideal condition of the human consciousness."[3] In other words Sassoon lacked the philosophy and architectonics against which to measure his experiences and comprehend them. He needed distance and objectivity. Righteous anger is simply too emotional for poetry. How little a noncombatant like Murry understood the nature of conflict and what was happening to those involved. How easy it was to dismiss, superciliously, a "popular" poet, one whose "popularity . . . may end by wrecking the real poetic gift which at rare intervals peeps out" (Murry, 74). Jealousy, of course, motivated the disdain for and attempted dismissal of the hero-poet. Committed to imagism, symbolism, and black verse, Murry could not appreciate satire, let alone sardonic existential angst reflecting a desperate search for meaning and convention in the absurdities of war. Sassoon, like other soldier-poets who survived, especially Graves and Blunden, would ever remain outside the canon of modernism.

Technique

It is obvious that the horror of trench combat, from the Battle of the Somme in 1916 on, matured Sassoon as man and artist, but it must also be recognized that the roots of his craft are Georgian, at least that part of the Georgian tradition which "culminated in the directness, brutality, and honesty of his best war verse" (Moore, 199). Clearly Sassoon's poetry contains no great technical innovations. Vivian de S. Pinto notes that Sassoon "used the smoothed rhyme decasyllabics of the Georgians in nearly all the poems and he seems to have learnt from Brooke's realistic poems the trick of producing a humorous effect by the contrast between a stately traditional metre and subject matter very unlike the dignified themes with which such metres are associated."[4] That is the point. The familiarity and control of the Georgian are juxtaposed with the horrors and terrors, the hypocrisy and mendacity, depicted by Sassoon. Without the form the public would have looked at Sassoon's accounts as the ravings of a shell-shocked victim. The juxtapositional binaries are the truth about the war and the unruffled life lived at home in Britain. Jon Silkin points out that "Another version of this technique is to juxtapose the language, or even the word, of common speech with the word of a previous, romanticized poetic diction, exposing thereby how much this diction and its underlying attitudes conflicted with the facts of mundane existence in general, but the war in particular."[5]

Whether employing juxtapositional metrics or diction, Sassoon exploits the variance and discordance between the apathy of the civilian population—his primary audience—and the sufferings of the soldiers. The sharp contrast of black and white served his palette well: the safe life at home and that of the short-lived species, the combat infantryman. Sassoon's motto could have been "Shove it in their faces!"

War Poetry Collections

Sassoon published four collections of war poems. *The Old Huntsman* (1917), dedicated to Thomas Hardy, contains 72 poems, 34 of which had appeared in earlier collections, and "The Redeemer," which had appeared first in the *Cambridge Magazine,* the chief organ of sane intellectual pacifism during World War I, and then in a pamphlet reprint. *Counter-Attack* (1918), dedicated to Robert Ross, who had urged Sassoon to write satiric war verse, contains 39 poems, 5 of which—"Dreamers," "Base Details," "Does It Matter?," "Glory of Women," and "To Any Dead Officer"—had also appeared in the *Cambridge Magazine* and its reprints. *Picture-Show* (1919), in an edition of 200, was privately printed in Cambridge. It contains 34 new poems. The New York edition, published in 1920 by E. P. Dutton and dedicated to John Masefield, has 7 additional new poems. *The War Poems of Siegfried Sassoon* (1919) contains 64 poems: 61 from *The Old Huntsman, Counter-Attack,* and *Picture-Show,* and 3 new poems, "In an Underground Dressing-Station," "Atrocities," and "Return of the Heroes." The poems in these collections form the core of the Sassoon poetry canon.

The Old Huntsman and Other Poems

The Old Huntsman is a book of music and muscle. It looks to the past, to an England that had changed and to a literary tradition that had evolved. Simultaneously it looks at the present, at a country in violent conflict and a literature in upheaval. Sassoon's war poems are products of two modes: the precombat, "Happy Warrior" pieces, influenced by Rupert Brooke's sonnets and the realistic, even naturalistic portrayals of the agonies of soldiers. The early, weekend-in-the-country, affected Georgianisms like "Dream-Forest" and "Wonderment," from prewar collections, are in *The Old Huntsman* both as fillers and as sops to placate nationalistic critics sure to be hostile to satiric war poems defiantly published in wartime.

The transitional poem is the title piece, "The Old Huntsman," dedicated to the author's hunting companion Norman Loder. In it Sassoon employs the now-traditional Georgian realism popularized by Masefield, but he has "sharpened his eye for physical detail" (Moore, 204). As in *The Daffodil Murderer,* Sassoon again chooses an ordinary person from the working class for protagonist and narrator, while "poetic diction" gives way to a colloquial style.

Interestingly Sassoon believed that the long, blank-verse title piece, "The Old Huntsman," which he had written early in 1915, was more important than either the war poems or the lush romantic, lyrical pieces composed even earlier. In fact "The Old Huntsman" was a work of near desperation by a poet approaching age 30 who realized that he still had not found his own voice (Cohen, 179). Sassoon had also realized that the readership for childhood reveries, ghosts, goblins, dragons, and witches had diminished rapidly to say the least, given the events of 1914. As in *The Daffodil Murderer,* "The Old Huntsman" indicates Sassoon's growing concern and compassion for less fortunate human beings. Now he is genuinely attempting to get inside a character and portray him with sympathy and understanding. Although nature is still a source of beauty and inspiration, and Sassoon is writing in "The Old Huntsman" about hunting and riding to hounds, he is no longer preoccupied with poetic conventions. Subject is ascending; self is receding. The language of "The

Old Huntsman" is pellucidly clear, and the poem is easily accessible to any reader. Sassoon has envisioned an audience other than himself, an idea he garnered from the reception to *The Daffodil Murderer.*

In the 200 blank-verse lines of "The Old Huntsman" the persona, an old, professional master of horse-and-hound, retired from active life, now the lease-owner of a village pub named the Golden Fleece, and tired of his failing business, relives in his mind the great days of old in the field and stable, remembering joyous times and lost opportunities. Sassoon presents a dramatic monologue in the Browning tradition, while evincing his own image of the good life now passing. The persona even describes the "old Duke" whom he sometimes served as if Sassoon had grayed his own hair and looked in the mirror: "Tall and spare, / Clean-shaved and grey, with shrewd, kind eyes, that twinkled."[6] This is the image Sassoon grew into in old age as the squire of Heyetesbury.

The Old Huntsman has little respect for conventional religion, a characteristic of much Georgian verse. He says, "Religion beats me" (*OH,* 4). His dream of hell is a travesty. If consists of fields without foxes and with bad riders. Further, he knew some hounds that "were wise as half your saints" (*OH,* 7). The poem's crucial insight is piquant: "where's the use of life and being glad / If God's not in your gladness?" (*OH,* 7). For him and presumably for Sassoon God and gladness are to be found not in the parson's sermon in the church but in the individual human heart.

One other nonwar poem in *The Old Huntsman* is especially significant. "Morning Express" is a realistic poem for the period, reading almost like a 1930s piece by Stephen Spender or W. H. Auden, with its description of "the wind-swept platform, pinched and white" and the travelers who "stand in pools of wintry light" (*OH,* 56). Virginia Woolf singled out this poem as foreshadowing Sassoon's war poetry by means of the "solid and in its way beautiful catalogue of facts." It showed "an early vein of realism."[7]

The transformation of Sassoon's war poetry from Brookean jingoism to original and brilliant antiwar satires is easily documented in *The Old Huntsman.* The watershed for Sassoon was his experiences of 1916, first at the Fourth Army School for combat training at Flixecourt in the spring of 1916, where he attended the infamous lectures on "the spirit of the bayonet," and then at the cataclysmic Battle of the Somme, 1 July and after. Sassoon's war poetry prior to these early 1916 occurrences is in the prevailing "happy warrior" mode.

The most clearly patriotic poems were those republished in *The Old Huntsman* from *Morning-Glory*: "Brothers," "The Dragon and the Undying," "To Victory," "To His Dead Body," discussed in chapter 2. The newer happy-warrior pieces include "Absolution," "Before the Battle," "A Mystic as Soldier," "The Redeemer," and the controversial "The Kiss."

"Absolution" acclaims the comradeship of the young soldiers, "the happy legion" bonded in a great quest and "having claimed this heritage of heart, / What need we more, my comrades and my brothers?" (*OH*, 13). This is the poetic equivalent of working up Dutch courage: a dollop of bravado to hide fear and a terrible reality. "Absolutism" is "meditative poetry as opposed to the poetry of experience" (Lane, 22). Like Brooke's famous sonnets, the poem romanticizes war, making it out to be ennobling and liberating: "yet war has made us wise, / And, fighting for our freedom, we are free" (*OH*, 13).

"A Mystic as Soldier" expects to find "God in the strife" (*OH*, 20). "Before the Battle," written on 25 June 1916, five days before the battle of the Somme commenced, has the untested soldier persona scorn the war that has taken him from his contemplation of nature, and he calls on a "river of stars and shadows [to] lead me through the night" (*OH*, 75). Now he has "no need to pray" (*OH*, 75).

"The Kiss" is the most interesting of Sassoon's precombat war poems. It was inspired by the notorious "spirit of the bayonet" training-camp lecture of Colonel Campbell, VC, mentioned earlier. Despite Sassoon's later disclaimer, the poem was meant to be taken literally (Graves, 339). Sassoon addresses his weapons:

> To these I turn, in these I trust;
> Brother Lead and Sister Steel.
> To his blind power I make appeal;
> I guard her beauty clean from rust.
> . . . .
> Sweet Sister, grant your soldier this;
> That in good fury he may feel
> the body where he sets his heel
> Quail from your downward darting kiss.
>
> (*OH*, 21)

Later Sassoon claimed the poem as satire, a reading made plausible by the almost-erotic embracing of bullet and blade: "She glitters naked; cold and fair" (*OH*, 21). Clearly Sassoon tried to salvage a good poem whose intent was no longer acceptable for him and for the post-Somme and eventually postwar milieu, by diverting interpretation from jingoism to satire. Another possibility, however, is that the poem equivocates, that it is simultaneously patriotic and satiric, reflecting Sassoon's razor's edge ambivalence toward the war, as well as his natural fear a few weeks before going up the line to combat for the first time. Now one can see the poem deconstructing, the bravado and bluster undermined by the encoded satiric reading. After all, Sassoon waffled, quite understandably, of course. In 1917 he protested the war, and in 1918 he was once more killing Germans by the score.

"The Redeemer," a longer poem, "typifies the crusading spirit of 1915" (Thorpe, 17). The English soldier is "white and strong." He "loved his time like any simple chap, / Good days of work and sport and homely song" (OH, 23). But he also is Christ the Redeemer "shouldering his load of planks, so hard to bear" (OH, 23). Tommy's sacrifice and martyrdom are implied. This precombat poem is Kipling-like too, because the "white" soldier's burden is also "The White Man's Burden." Of course, the enemy is white too, but that fact is ignored as the British are fighting to save civilization, at least in their own adducing. Only later will Sassoon, having seen the German corpses, recognize shared humanity and the democracy of death.

Until the last stanza "The Redeemer" is calm and prosaic. Then Sassoon employs, perhaps for the first time, the juxtaposition of a startlingly ironic ending to a seemingly conventional patriotic lyric. Simultaneously Sassoon's compassion for the common soldier, men he will soon lead to mutilation and death, is born:

> Then the flame sank, and all grew black as pitch,
> While we began to struggle along the ditch;
> And someone flung his burden in the muck,
> Mumbling: "Oh Christ Almighty, now I'm stuck!"
>
> (OH, 24)

The soldiers are now victims. They are stuck indeed, trapped in the flame and black of hell. And Christ becomes a blasphemy.

The combat poems in *The Old Huntsman* introduce the immortal Sassoon, the poems on which a generation of British schoolchildren, especially boys in public (fee-paying) schools, grew up.[8] Sassoon is no longer merely "a Georgian in uniform."[9] Now his diction is direct, unsentimental, objective, colloquial, and blunt; his subjects, nasty, brutal, bitter, and horrible. The ineffable must be said. The intolerable must be exposed.

"When I'm among a Blaze of Lights" is a tirade against the earthy pleasures of Sassoon's fellow officers, who, when the persona is enjoying an anodyne of remembrance of nature and good books, come up to him at the "cocktail bar" and say, "Another drink?" (*OH,* 18). The ascetic, perhaps prudish Sassoon seldom felt a part of a group. He was the proverbial outsider, able to make an individual friend but never comfortable with the many, whose common enjoyments, including "women dawdling through delights, . . . turns my living heart to stone" (*OH,* 18).

"Golgotha" continues the Christ-soldier iterative image, but Sassoon's imagery has grown more startling, as if the Elizabethan had suddenly turned Jacobean: "The sentry keeps his watch where no one stirs / But the brown rats, the nimble scavengers" (*OH,* 19). This last sentence of a short poem confirms Sassoon's adoption of the punch-to-the-solar-plexus ending.

"A Whispered Tale" lauds "the good, simple soldier, seasoned well" (*OH,* 30). "A Subaltern" is a gentle, touching description of a very young officer "Dreaming about his girl" as he confides, man to man, with the persona in the trenches. But the girl has "no place in Hell" (*OH,* 25). Embarrassed by the giving of his confidence, "'Good God!' he laughed, and calmly filled his pipe, / Wondering why he always talked such tripe" (*OH,* 25). "In the Pink" depicts the thoughts of an officer-censor scanning the letters to home written by his men. He reads between the lines: "So Davis wrote: 'This leaves me in the pink,'" but Willie Davis knows and is thinking that "tomorrow night we trudge / Up to the trenches, and my boots are rotten" (*OH,* 26). The officer-persona ruminates: "Tonight he's in the pink; but soon he'll die. / And still the war goes on; *he* don't know why" (*OH,* 26). It is Sassoon, of course, who no longer knows "why." Neither officer nor enlistee comprehends the reasons for the continuation of the war, but Sassoon has now chosen to make the mute, suffering private soldier his hero. Concomitantly the soldier poets—Sassoon and others—become, for that part of British society truly understanding of what was really happening to a generation of young men, "the only possible social hero . . . the writer who has suffered with the soldiers and who relates the idiocy of the war."[10]

In "A Working Party," a longer poem, the enlisted soldier-hero—a "young man with a meagre wife / And two pale children in a Midland town" (*OH,* 28) who likes to show their photograph to all his mates—is killed, ironically, as he tries to make the trench more secure. In other words he has been acting as a protector and a nurturer rather than as a killer, but "the instant split / His startled life with lead, and all went out" (*OH*, 29). Carried to the rear, he is now "a jolting lump / Beyond all tenderness and care" (*OH*, 29). Pity sets in with rigor mortis. Death is swallowing both experience and poetry. Meanwhile the readers of 1917 "enjoy" a vicarious participation and a distant moral indignation at the mindlessness and waste of the war, but this is an uncomfortable position for those who think through to their complicity and hypocrisy.

"Blighters" is one of Sassoon's most famous war poems. In it "Sassoon's expression of his hatred for excessive patriotism approaches the rabid."[11] Patriotic flatulence disgusted him. The eight-line poem presaged Joan Littlewood's savage musical satire *Oh What a Lovely War* (1963), a work implying that World War I was less real to the British civilian population than its representations on the music hall stages. In the poem's music hall setting "The House is crammed" with grinning, cackling patrons. The "prancing ranks / Of harlots shrill the chorus drunk with din" (*OH*, 31). The persona longs for a tank to clear out the house so "there'd be no more jokes in Music-halls / To mock the riddled corpses round Bapaume" (*OH*, 31), where Sassoon and his men were fighting and dying. Sassoon is, however, grossly unfair to the poor women of the chorus, who were entertainers, not harlots, although his general indignation and frustration are justifiable.

"At Carnoy" was written on 3 July 1916, three days into the Somme offensive. Now Sassoon is writing poetry in the middle of the greatest and most costly battle in British military history, and he is angry with God, for "To-morrow we must go / To take some curse'd Wood. . . . O world God made!" (*OH*, 32).

Like a "New Elizabethan," as some Georgians styled themselves, Sassoon, in "Two Hundred Years After," writes a miniature history play of the future. A Frenchman in the twenty-second century "one winter night" sees English ghosts, a rations party with a wagon and mules moving to the long-obliterated front. He tells his story to an old man who has also "seen soldiers pass along that hill" (*OH*, 34). With simple words, sounding as if they came from the pen of Hardy or Housman, the old man commiserates: "Poor silent things, they were the English dead / Who came to fight in France and got their fill" (*OH*, 34). The clarity and extreme economy of the literal imagery are brilliant.

"They" is another of the famous Sassoon war poems. Here Sassoon "launches an attack . . . on the apparent subservience of the Anglican church to the state, and on the windy rhetoric that was one of the main civilian contributions to the war"[12]:

> The Bishop tells us: "When the boys come back
> They will not be the same; for they'll have fought
> In a just cause: they lead the last attack
> On Anti-Christ."
>
> *(OH, 35)*

But the soldiers' reply to this cant is filled with angry scorn:

> "We're none of us the same!" the boys reply.
> "For George lost both his legs; and Bill's stone blind;
> Poor Jim's shot through the lungs and like to die;
> And Bert's gone siphilitic"
>
> *(OH, 35)*

Once more Sassoon is driving home the raw truths of war to civilians. He believed that this was the first time a reference to syphilis had appeared in English poetry. Of course, he was working in the naturalistic mode of Georgian poetry. If Masefield could use "bloody," he would use words like "siphilitic." Edward Marsh showed courage himself when he included the poem in *Georgian Poetry 1916–1917,* because the mere mention of syphilis was considered an offense against public decorum and the poem an affront to the public's patriotism. Yet most readers then, as now, were carried along by the emotion and sympathized with the poet's contempt, indignation, and hatred.

In "Stand-to: Good Friday Morning" the disgruntled infantryman in the trench sardonically offers Jesus a deal:

> O Jesus, send me a wound to-day,
> And I'll believe in Your bread and wine,
> And get my bloody old sins washed white!
>
> *(OH, 36)*

The reductive irony is complete. The soldier's bargain is blasphemy. He knows that Jesus, on the day of his crucifixion, has neither thought for a soldier's misery and desperation nor hope for his despair.

"Special-Constable," "The Choral Union," and "Liquor Control"—this last an allegorical attack on government control of spirits consumption, ironically dedicated to Roderick Meiklejohn, a senior treasury official and one of Robbie Ross's circle—are all weak poems apparently written on leave. "Special-Constable" attacks the petty tyranny of civilian defense personnel. "The Choral Union" has a drunk mistaking an evangelical prayer meeting for a music hall show and thinking he has somehow died and gone to heaven. It is not a very successful attempt at humor.

There are no palliatives for the disease of war. "The One-Legged Man" is overjoyed that now, "Safe with his wound," he has returned to be "a citizen of life," for "Thank God they had to amputate!" (OH, 43). If a soldier blesses a mutilation that takes him from the front, how terrible his experience must have been. The unspoken but implied horror is the power of the poem. Sassoon has learned to write between the lines.

"Enemies" is an autobiographical sonnet in which the persona's dead friend's ghost, presumably Sassoon's friend David Thomas, looks on the slaughtered "German that I shot / When for his death my brooding rage was hot" (OH, 44). The dead friend feels no anger or bitterness now. Instead his angelic face "could lead them out of hell" (OH, 44). The poem's strength is in its flat, discursive style and consequent avoidance of "lost buddy" sentimentality.

"The Tomb-Stone Maker" complains to the persona that too many people—he means soldiers—are dying out of England, and thus he notes, with accidental irony, "Unless the fighting stops I'll soon be broke" (OH, 45). He offers his lament while leaning "Against a sorrowing angel's breast" (OH, 45). Further, the stonecutter deplores the fact that the soldiers are now "buried in such wretched style." The persona teases him by declaring that the "Germans boil dead soldiers down for fat" (OH, 45), and the stonecutter believes him, shocked at the "shameful sin" of it. Again the irony is in the unstated realization that the stonecutter is mainly concerned with his loss of business.

"Arms and the Man" lays heavy guilt on the reader. When Sassoon sings of "Arms and the Man," he, unlike Virgil, refers not to glory but to amputated limbs. Wounded "Captain Croesus" goes to a military doctor in the hope of getting his medical leave prolonged even though "his wound was healed and mended" (OH, 46). In the waiting room he sees a notice informing amputees where they can get arms and legs. A price scale is included, but "officers could get them free" (OH, 46).

Delirious, a mortally wounded soldier dies in the 12-line poem "Died of Wounds." His business now is dying, and "he did his business well" (OH, 47). With a surrealistic double-image use of metonymy, the poem ends: "next morning he was dead / And some Slight Wound lay smiling on his bed" (OH, 47). Sassoon quite well understands the psychology of surviving, how one is secretly and often guiltily glad that it is not he or she who has died. In this case it is a slightly wounded soldier who is glad he has not been chosen by the red god Mars, but the stunned reader cannot help but first envision a detached wound on a bed.

The superb poem "The Hero," a satire of circumstance, is both sardonic and sentimental. In it a white-haired, grieving mother is given, by a brother officer, a fictitious account of her cowardly officer-son's death in battle. The three-stanza, 18-line narrative poem is tightly packed with quick-sketch characterizations of the mother and three officers. The mother is deluded by the visiting fellow officer, who "told the poor old dear some gallant lies," and by the colonel, who "writes so nicely" (*OH*, 48). She is foolishly proud that her son had "been so brave, her glorious boy" (*OH*, 48). The truth is that the young officer had panicked, had "tried to get sent home," and was "Blown to small bits" (*OH*, 48). The fellow officer actually thinks the son, Jack, was a "cold-footed, useless swine" (*OH*, 48). "The Hero" clearly depicts the conflicting loyalties in Sassoon. He has contempt for all parties involved in the tragic farce of false reportage, but he has pity too for the mother, the son, and the burdened messenger. We are even sorry for the tough colonel, who, after all, has a miserable duty to perform. Jack is pitied because he suffered terrible mental anguish and died horribly, yet the reader also joins the persona in some feeling of contempt for his poor showing as a soldier when his comrades needed him. Early in his combat infantry experience Sassoon typically had little understanding of male hysteria and how in battle thousands of soldiers "lost their voices and spoke with their bodies. . . . Shell shock," says Elaine Showalter, "was the body language of masculine complaint."[13] As time passed Sassoon and others understood better.

The mother in "The Hero" is pitied for her loss and disdained for her ignorance, credulity, and susceptibility to male manipulation. She has bought into patriarchal values, the very values that have taken her son from her. The fellow officer is pitied because he has to lie in comforting the old woman, and we also pity him for the way the war has hardened him. "The Hero" is an excellent example of the emotional ambiguity that resides behind Sassoon's war poetry, despite "the technical conservatism and intellectual simplicity of the poems" (Onions, 42). The conservatism and simplicity, however, facilitated mass communication and served propagandistically. After all, Sassoon, as prophet-poet, is constrained to warn as many people as possible of the horror and futility of war, even while realizing, with great frustration, that the public could never truly comprehend the incredible reality of battle.

"Stretcher Case," dedicated to Edward Marsh, depicts a sedated, badly wounded soldier awakening on the medical train taking him back to

"Blighty," the British soldier's term for England, reachable only by means of a "blighty," a serious enough wound to warrant evacuation. Now the ingenuous evacuee dreams of his unchanging and reliable friends at home: "Lung Tonic, Mustard, Liver Pills and Beer" (*OH,* 50). "Conscripts" is a satiric allegory in which a drill-sergeant persona drives the social graces from his recruits. He sees his wards as personifications of "Joy," "Wisdom," "Fancy," "Enchantment," and "Romance." Although his duty is to pound individuality out of them, he still sees them as individual human beings. The "common ones that I despised" survive, but "most of those I'd loved too well got killed" (*OH,* 52). Despite the allegory and the abstraction, the poem is too personal to work. The sensibility portrayed is clearly not a drill sergeant's but an officer-poet's.

"The Road" is a sentimentalized narrative about an exhausted Scottish soldier too weary to realize that a woman refugee is embracing and comforting him. The weak poem "Secret Music" insists that "the roar of guns" will not "destroy my life" (*OH,* 54) or the joy of music. "Before the Battle," written on 25 June 1916, five days before the Battle of the Somme, finds the persona with "no need to pray" and scorning "the growl and rumble of the fight" (*OH,* 75). "The Last Meeting" is an elegy to David Thomas. Unfortunately, it is ruined by a lush, romantic, overly ornate style that drowns the subject by drawing too much attention to itself. The long poem is also too full of "I"s, as if the persona is jostling for primacy of place with the dead friend. Clichés abound—"I know that he is lost among the stars" (*OH,* 103), the sky is "tranquil," the "voice of doom . . . crackles overhead," and so on. The attempt to immortalize the essence or spirit of his friend, in imitation of Shelley's *Adonais,* fails, although Sassoon will continue to deplore the cruel selectivity of the war that killed off the young, the fittest, and the finest (Silkin, 143–44).

The last poem in *The Old Huntsman,* "A Letter Home," is dedicated to Robert Graves and is in fact a letter written to his army comrade. The raison d'être for the "Letter" is that Sassoon cannot shake his grief for David Thomas and feels that Graves too must miss "One whose yellow head was kissed / By the gods, who thought about him / Till they couldn't do without him" (*OH,* 107). Sassoon envisions "Soldier David" singing madrigals. Alas, the poem is maudlin, too specifically personal, lacking distance and perspective, and dripping with sentimentality. On the other hand, Sassoon is truly suffering greatly over the loss of a loved one, and he is affirming the former existence on earth of his dear young friend by communing with Graves, who knew Thomas and understands how war destroys the brave and the beautiful.

Because the poem was of such great personal importance to him, Sassoon placed the five-stanza-long "A Letter Home" at the end of his first book-length collection for public sale. It is significant too that Sassoon ends the poem and the book on a note of optimism, perhaps "facile optimism" (Thorpe, 28). The persona watches "the spark / Lit to guide me; for I know / Dreams will triumph" (*OH*, 108–9).

Poems like "A Letter Home" and "The Last Meeting" illustrate the eternal dilemma for sensitive military people, especially the citizen-soldier, for whom military life and the requirement to do violence in the name of the state are terrible if temporary imperatives. The military life provokes a love-hate response. That life in wartime, dangerous and intense, wherein one relies for survival on others and lives closer to comrades than wives and husbands do, has a powerful hold on thoroughly decent human beings despite what they are often called on to do. Perhaps that is why Sassoon continued to allow himself the appellation Captain Sassoon long after his war had ended.

The war poems in *The Old Huntsman* are rough stuff: tough poems for a tough time. At their most effective they terrify, shock, and numb. Sassoon's pain and indignation are so real that our pity for him makes up for his lack of compassion in those poems which attack clergy and civilians. His pity, grief, and love are reserved for his fellow soldiers, especially the ranker, for whom trench warfare meant suffering, mutilation, and death. Simple, concise, pointed, descriptive, and acrid, the poems provided the author with an opportunity for catharsis and a refined recording, a distillation of what went into his diaries. Terrible experiences needed to be written out of the mind, banished to paper. D. J. Enright is correct in stating that, at least for his combat poetry, Sassoon's most interesting work revolves around the so-called "negative emotions—horror, anger, and disgust."[14] The process was for purgation. What was red before his eyes had to be given time and place to grow green in memory.

Counter-Attack and Other Poems

Between the publication of *The Old Huntsman* and *Counter-Attack,* Sassoon's most memorable and powerful collection of poetry, the poet underwent the ordeal of his singular revolt against the continuation of the war. He had become a hero of war and then a hero of peace. This role fit into an existing tradition, for "The poet or artist as hero is obviously a central notion of Romanticism" (Onions, 35). In the West authority is often earned by action. Sometimes, as in the case of Vaclav Havel, for example, it is granted for moral and courageous artistry. In "A Defence of Poetry" Shelley asserts the supreme value of poets, claiming, immortally, that "Poets are the unacknowledged legislators of the world." Sassoon, the poet-warrior, self-seconded as poet-legislator against the war, was under treatment, allegedly for shell shock, in Craiglockhart Hospital when he wrote most of the poems in *Counter-Attack*. While there he read one of the most significant books written during and about World War I, Henri Barbusse's *Le Feu*, which appeared in 1916 and was translated into English in 1917 by Fitzwater Wray as *Under Fire*. Barbusse, a wounded, hospitalized French combat soldier and Marxist, wrote a starkly realistic novel about how the war and militaristic nations victimized soldiers. For Barbusse, war is the ultimate exploitation of humankind, and its greatest effect is depravity. Sassoon read *Le Feu* in French and then lent his copy to Wilfred Owen. It set both men on fire. They saw how battle impression and reportage could be turned to art. Thus *Le Feu* is a work of great importance to English war poetry. Sassoon recognized his debt to Barbusse by including a long quotation from *Le Feu* as an epigraph to *Counter-Attack*.

In *Counter-Attack*, dedicated to Robert Ross and devoid of Georgian pastorals, Sassoon brings his targets into sharper focus and sustains consistency by continued use of metronomic meters and familiar forms. Directness is paramount. In Sassoon's most significant collection abstraction and allegory are nearly totally banished. *Counter-Attack* rails against the institutions of the establishment: the church, the state, the army, and the general staff. Sassoon's old chief target, the civilian population, is still in his sights. The assault on the military leadership, an extramural government in itself, brought the censor's wrath and nearly caused a refusal of publication (Crawford, 124). The poems of *Counter-Attack* deeply disturbed the public. The experiences that inspired the collection haunted Sassoon all his life and have haunted readers of poetry ever since.

The opening lines of *Counter-Attack*, in the poem "'Prelude: The Troops,' reveal a stricken world whose inhabitants have been overwhelmed by some unspeakable disaster" (Johnston, 96):

> Dim, gradual thinning of the shapeless gloom
> Shudders to drizzling daybreak that reveals
> Disconsolate men who stamp their sodden boots
> And turn dulled, sunken faces to the sky
> Haggard and hopeless.[15]

The troops are survivors of the Deluge; they are men of "The Waste Land." Their lives are a gross nightmare as they "Cling to life with stubborn hands" (*C-A,* 9). In the end they are "The unreturning army that was youth" (*C-A,* 10). This single, deft phrase strikes the chord of pity architectonic to the collection.

The title poem, "Counter-Attack," is a narrative depicting the chaotic effect of a German counterattack on a section of their own former front line captured by the British "hours before / While dawn broke like a face with blinking eyes" (*C-A,* 11). The most gruesome description in the entire Sassoon canon follows the opening report of the seizure of the trench:

> The place was rotten with dead; green clumsy legs
> High booted, sprawled and grovelled along the saps;
> And trunks, face downward, in the sucking mud,
> Wallowed like trodden sand-bags loosely filled;
> And naked sodden buttocks, mats of hair,
> Bulged, clotted heads slept in the plastering slime.
> And then the rain began,—the jolly old rain!
>
> (*C-A,* 11)

Even rain! The last obscenity and indignity. The anointing of misery. The ensuing counterattack becomes a shambles, and the reader is drawn from a generalized narration into experiencing the poem as an infantryman fighting for his life, which, after a wound and flopping around the trench, he loses from loss of blood. In a mere 39 lines the entire skirmish is presented, like cinema, in unfolding literal images. "Counter-Attack" is the storyboard of battle.

In "The Rear-Guard (Hindenberg Line, April 1917)" an exhausted British officer is looking for battalion headquarters in a captured tunnel, when, in the dark and wreckage, he stumbles across a soldier seemingly asleep: "Get up and guide me through this stinking place" (*C-A,* 14). There is no response. "Savage, he kicked a soft, unanswering heap" (*C-A,* 14). The light from his flashlight reveals a 10-day-old corpse still showing the agony of death on its face, and the persona, "with sweat of horror in his hair" (*C-A,* 15), staggers out of the hellish tunnel into the twilight. "The Rear-Guard" shows Sassoon getting control over his material, just as a soldier must have control over his or her situation. Graphic depiction is a method of controlling that situation and one's own self. Significantly the nationality of the dead soldier is not stated. The officer has spoken English to the corpse, thinking the dead soldier was asleep, but the corpse was part of the sacrificed "rear-guard" and thus a German. Death is an equal opportunity employer. It provides inimical soldiers with an instant initiation into comradeship.

"Wirers" depicts the laying of barbed wire in no-man's-land, an extremely dangerous job, often done at high cost of brave lives. Sassoon, however, does not dwell on individual bravery; he takes it for granted. Cowardice is the exception. In "Wirers"

> Young Hughes was badly hit; I heard him carried away,
> Moaning at every lurch; no doubt he'll die to-day.
> But *we* can say the front-line wire's been safely mended.
>
> (*C-A*, 17)

The important effect, of course, is the irony, not Hughes's courage in no-man's-land. As an antiwar propagandist, Sassoon cannot allow the war any moral significance, even a soldier's personal response to "the imperatives of duty" (Johnston, 102). The experience of war is totally without value, except perhaps for whatever art it engenders. Death in war is routine and matter-of-fact, paradoxically, as life is in peace.

"Attack" again didactically insists on the facts and details of war, just as Sassoon's model, Hardy, had "pessimistically" insisted on a realistic portrayal of life. Here the British assault, the soldiers, grenades, guns, tanks, and even the newfangled wristwatch—"time ticks blank and busy on their wrists" (*C-A*, 18)—are presented in detail, until the personification and the prayer of the last two lines, in which "hope, with furtive eyes and grasping fists, / Flounders in mud. O Jesu, make it stop!" (*C-A*, 18). The persona, in extremis, cries out, but Jesus does not interfere, perhaps does not care.

"Dreamers," a sonnet, contrasts the reality of life in the trenches, presented in the octave, with the dreams of the soldiers, presented in the sestet. The soldiers dream of "Bank-holidays, and picture shows, and spats, / And going to the office in the train" (*C-A*, 19). All they want is the ordinary life from which they were wrenched by the war. "Dreamers" contains one of Sassoon's most famous lines, "Soldiers are citizens of death's grey land" (*C-A*, 19).

"How to Die"'s ironic message results from the bitter irony of the poem's two stanzas. The first depicts a soldier's death as it might be presented in a sentimental painting or a poem written by a civilian. He dies radiant and happy, "on his lips a whispered name" (*C-A*, 20). In the second stanza the persona mockingly complains that some civilians think soldiers "go West with sobs and curses," when in fact "they've been taught the way to do it," presumably vicariously by staff officers, "like Christian soldiers . . . passing through it / With due regard for decent taste" (*C-A*, 20). The poem's last sentence illustrates a technique for a slam closing by incorporating a cliché about dying—"passing through it"—as an indictment of the civilian audience. It thinks in untrue clichés. In mocking the banal conception of death in battle, Sassoon willfully lays a heavy burden of guilt on those who support the war but do not participate in it.

"The Effect" begins with a headnote in which a war correspondent lauds the effect of a British bombardment laid on German troops. "The effect of our bombardment was terrific. One man told me that he had never seen so many dead before" (*C-A*, 21). The Germans are dealt with by the press as statistics, but Sassoon insists that humans are humans. He establishes this by shifting from the collective "dead" to the palpable reality behind the headlines and the ignorant journalism, namely that "Dick" was killed last week, "Flapping along the fire-step like a fish" (*C-A*, 21). The bitter poem ends with a fishmonger's cry: *"Who'll buy my nice fish corpses, two for a penny?"* (*C-A*, 22). How cheap can death get?

Poems like "Twelve Months After" indicate the great loyalty that existed between combat officers and their men in the British army on the western front. Battallion officers were father figures and older brothers to rankers in their outfits, many of whom were considerably older than the platoon and company officers who commanded them. In "Twelve Months After" the officer-persona sees or dreams of his old platoon. They muster for him. Then the poem is broken by a line of asterisks, and time or the dream has passed. A marching song is heard: "Old soldiers never die; they simply fide a-why!" (*C-A*, 23). The persona tells us that the song is what they used to sing on the road in France "Before the last push began." In typical Sassoon fashion the last, unexpected line—"That's where they are today, knocked over to a man" (*C-A*, 23)—knocks over the reader. Sassoon really was cruelest of all to ordinary civilian readers—mothers, fathers, sisters, wives of soldiers—trying to warn and educate them. Whenever he could, he dumped the bloody corpses on their doorsteps.

"The Fathers," snug in their club, "Gross, goggle-eyed," and wheezing, live their lives through the "adventures" of their soldier-sons, as if the young men were playing sports. They are blissfully unaware of the reality of their sons' precarious lives. The poem is like a satiric cartoon in *Punch.* The persona, like the reader, "watches them toddle through the door— / These impotent old friends of mine" (*C-A*, 24). Sassoon's many middle-aged establishment friends must have chafed under the depiction of their hollowness and insensibility toward the facts of the war and the lengthy casualty lists. Sassoon was unwilling to spare even his patrons and promoters.

"Base Details" is another attack on old men, this time senior officers safe at rear bases, but "fierce, and bald, and short of breath" (C-A, 25), hardly warrior material. In World War II this type of miles gloriosus was called a Colonel Blimp. The persona pretends he would like to be an old staff officer and "live with scarlet Majors at the Base" (C-A, 25). They are "scarlet Majors" because they wear red tabs as staff officers and because they are red-faced, blustering, puffed-up male birds. The persona, obviously a serving trench soldier, sardonically says that were he an old staffer, he would "speed glum heroes up the line to death" and when the war was over "toddle safely home and die—in bed" (C-A, 25). The incompetence, insensitivity, and decadence of senior officers is a major theme in Sassoon's war poems. Sassoon hated the idea that some men had to fight and die, while others in uniform had safe, cushy jobs. It is the eternal grievance of the combat soldier against rear-echelon troops, whom he or she sees as shirkers and parasites.

Sassoon excels as an ironist in "The Fathers," "Base Details," and "The General." In the last a kindly, paternal leader greets the men going into the line with "Good-morning; good-morning!" as if they were passing in a street. "Harry" and "Jack" liked him—"He's a cheery old card" (C-A, 26)—but they are dead now because "he did for them both by his plan of attack" (C-A, 26). Again Sassoon drives home his attack, this time on the notoriously incompetent British generals, with a shocking last line.

"Lamentations" is the antithesis to "The Hero" in *The Old Huntsman*. Now the blooded Sassoon has more sympathy for the "shell-shocked," traumatized soldier suffering the eruption of his grief over the news of his brother's death in battle. He "raved at the bleeding war. . . . Moaned, shouted, sobbed, and choked, while he was kneeling / Half naked on the floor" (C-A, 27). This time Sassoon keeps an ironist's distance, and the persona is another officer, one who is insensitive to his comrade's suffering. Coldly and precisely he comments, "In my belief / Such men have lost all patriotic feeling" (C-A, 27). As planned, the reader is shocked by the emotional distance of the persona from the sufferer. Was Sassoon thinking of his own, early war reaction to the death of his younger brother at Gallipoli as perhaps documented in the patriotic "Brothers"?

"Does It Matter?" ironically downplays the loss of a leg, "For people will always be kind"; the loss of sight, for "There's such splendid work for the blind"; or even shell shock, for "You can drink and forget" (*C-A,* 28). The poem ends in open sarcasm: "And no one will worry a bit" (*C-A,* 28). The absurd consolations offered by the civilian establishment for wounds and maiming deserve the mocking scorn they receive.

"Fight to a Finish," an infantryman's fantasy, is a vicious, angry attack on the press and the government. Sassoon's own regiment, the Royal Welch Fusiliers, at the future parade of those "who'd refrained from dying," fix bayonets and charge the "Yellow-Pressmen," those jingoistic, dishonest, and cowardly journalists, and while they are grunting and squeaking like stuck pigs, the persona's "trusty bombers," with their hand grenades, go on "To clear those Junkers out of Parliament" (*C-A,* 29). To Sassoon the members of Parliament are no different from the enemy's aristocrats. For the furious soldiers "This moment is their finest" (*C-A,* 29), not the welcome-home parade.

"Fight to a Finish" also indicates Sassoon's growing if not fully articulated socialism. The visualized attack on Parliament is a coded call for revolution, a dream of vengeful soldiers, as in Russia in 1917 and Germany, Austria, and Turkey late in 1918, attempting to destroy the institutions that betrayed them.

"Editorial Impressions" is another attack on the jingoistic press, "certain 'all was going well'" (*C-A,* 30) and that the troops were in high morale, based on quick visits to the trenches. In the punch line a "severely wounded" soldier sardonically comments, "Ah, yes, but it's the Press that leads the way!" (*C-A,* 30).

The depiction in "Suicide in the Trenches" of "a simple soldier boy" is derivative of A. E. Housman. The sensitive young soldier is unable to bear conditions in the trenches, and he "put a bullet through his brain" (*C-A,* 31). "Suicide in the Trenches" is "Sassoon's most blatant lapse into propaganda" (Crawford, 126), because he does not let the unfortunate story speak for itself as an objective correlative. Instead he editorializes. The last stanza accuses:

> You snug-faced crowds with kindling eye
> Who cheer when soldier lads march by,
> Sneak home and pray you'll never know
> The hell where youth and laughter go.
>
> (*C-A,* 31)

Sassoon's combat soldiers are seldom fierce and most often depicted as passive victims of circumstances beyond their control. Unheroic, only human, they are no masculine stereotypes of courage, strength, and stoicism. Instead they succumb to depression, stress, hysteria, and suicide, while being driven like khaki sheep to slaughter.

"Glory of Women" and "Their Frailty" unfairly attack women as shallow, pliant, manipulated, and narrow of vision. Sassoon apparently disliked women in general and could not see or understand their sufferings over the loss of loved ones, their painful sojourns of waiting, and that they were no more easily controlled by censorship and propaganda than men or indeed even the troops were. Women were the most passive afflicted of the war, but Sassoon fell into the trap of blaming the victim. Clearly false assumptions about heroism in war and "Chocolate Soldiers" are not the special province of women. Not all, and probably very few, are "By tales of dirt and danger fondly thrilled" (C-A, 32), even though notions of courage and privation are generally valorized in wartime. The endless knitting of socks and comforters that Sassoon derides is a method of suppressing anxiety. At least Sassoon implicitly recognizes the sisterhood of women whose sons are at war:

> O German mother dreaming by the fire,
> While you are knitting socks to send your son
> His face is trodden deeper in the mud.
>
> (C-A, 32)

The woman in the first stanza of "The Frailty" is glad her male, whether husband, son, or lover, has "got a Blighty wound" (C-A, 33). In the second stanza he is back in France, and so now she prays for peace. In the third stanza Sassoon reveals the "truth" about women: they "don't care / So long as He's all right" (C-A, 33). Woman can merely comprehend the significance of the war in selfish personal terms, in how it affects them through the men of their lives who are in the army. Sassoon's tone in "Glory of Women" and "Their Frailty" is mean. For a sensitive poet and a gay man, Sassoon's attack on women is surprising, but it is also somewhat in keeping with the traditional paternalistic attitudes of his class and his milieu.

"The Hawthorn Tree" is a pedestrian love lyric with the persona pining for a "lad that's out in France / With fearsome things to see" (C-A, 34). Nevertheless the poem provides a refreshing break from the suffering and brutality that surrounds it in the collection. It has some of the directness and simplicity of D. H. Lawrence's verse but not the depth or the resonance.

"The Investiture" takes place in Heaven, where "God with a Roll of Honour in His Hand / Sits welcoming the heroes who have died" (*C-A*, 35). Then the persona's lover or friend enters, "Wearing a blood-soaked bandage on [his] head" (*C-A*, 35). Although Heaven is a grand place, the dead soldier is alone and lonely without the persona, who in his anger at the death of the hero exclaims, "If I were there we'd snowball Death with skulls" (*C-A*, 35), a very Jacobean image. The poem's conceits are too extravagant, and the mythical depiction of God, angels, and Heaven detracts from the ghostly, elegiac intent.

"Autumn," a throwback to conventional imagery and Sassoon's prewar, Pre-Raphaelite style, is also a lament for "martyred youth and manhood overthrown" (*C-A*, 48), and "Invocation" calls on the dead lover in Heaven to "teach my soul to wake" (*C-A*, 49) and bring beauty down from Heaven. "The Triumph" seems out of place, reverting to earlier "poetic" language like "the terrible flickering gloom" (*C-A*, 54).

Conversational in style but hysterical in intensity, "Repression of War Experience" concerns self-communing. The persona is attempting to drive out thoughts of combat, where men, like moths to a candle's flame, "blunder in / And scorch their wings with glory, liquid flame" (*C-A*, 51). In his psychotic world there "are crowds of ghosts among the trees" (*C-A*, 52), but these are not ghosts of soldiers; they are in France. Instead these are "horrible shapes in shrouds . . . old men with ugly souls, / Who wore their bodies out with nasty sins" (*C-A*, 52). In a distracted, melodramatic monologue, the persona, far from the front, hears the sound of guns and the thud of shells: "I'm going stark, staring mad because of the guns" (*C-A*, 53). The poem's attack on the war and old civilian men again is unfocused and the effect stagy and unconvincing.

"Survivors," written at Craiglockhart Hospital in October 1917, devises a persona who optimistically discusses shell-shocked patients without understanding their experiences or their plight. The brilliant literal imagery of the poem is in the lines describing the suffering of the victims, who are now "Children, with eyes that hate you, broken and mad" (*C-A*, 55). The fatuous persona, perhaps a physician, has only bromides to offer: "No doubt they'll soon get well. . . . Of course they're 'longing to go out again'" (*C-A*, 55).

In "Joy-Bells" Sassoon again is sarcastic toward the church and churchmen because their bells, ringing in patriotic fervor, "changed us into soldiers" (*C-A*, 56). Now, in the war, the bells are useless and their metal needed for guns. Still, "Fierce-browed prelates" safe at home "proclaim / That if our Lord returned He'd fight for *us*" (*C-A*, 56). Sassoon wants the bishops laboring in the war effort too: "Shoulder to shoulder with the motor bus" (*C-A*, 56). For Sassoon and for Owen, Christ was already there in the trenches in the mass martyrdom occurring.

"Remorse" presents the persona in the eternal moral dilemma of soldiery: how can it be right to kill in cold blood? He remembers "how he saw the German run, Screaming for mercy among the stumps of trees. . . . Our chaps were sticking them like pigs" (*C-A*, 57). He wonders how he can tell his father of the terrible things he has done: "there's things in war one dare not tell" (*C-A*, 57).

"Dead Musicians" and "The Dream," both written at Craiglockhart, evince a mind preoccupied with death. In the former the persona eschews the power of classical musicians, such as Bach, Mozart, and Beethoven, artists who once "built cathedrals in my heart" (*C-A*, 58). Now the persona wants "fox-trot tunes" and ragtime, to bring back the ghosts of dead friends. But then "the song breaks off; and I'm alone. / They're dead. . . . For God's sake stop the gramophone" (*C-A*, 59). The sad poem deeply pains the reader too. "The Dream" once more has Sassoon remembering the enlisted men who served under him. He is filled with "Burning bitterness / That I must take them to the accursed line" (*C-A*, 61) and feed them "To the foul beast of war that bludgeons life" (*C-A*, 62). "The Dream" fully expresses the frustration and helplessness of those with responsibilities to others in a meat-grinder war.

In the Kiplingesque "In Barracks" Sassoon sentimentalizes the recruits, bidding them, "Sleep well, you lusty Fusiliers" (*C-A*, 63), not willing to admit that later he would put many to bed with a shovel. "Together," the last poem in *Counter-Attack*, is another ghost poem. The persona is remembering his dead friend, who ghostly gallops with him on a spectral ride. And so *Counter-Attack* ends with David Thomas's spirit saying, "at the stable-door . . . good-night" (*C-A*, 64). Painful though it was, Sassoon earned dividends from the emotional investment of his deep mourning for Thomas and other lost soldiers whom he loved. The paroxysms of grief were perhaps surrogate for and relief from the submerged, repressed, and encrypted feelings of grief for the death of his youthful, handsome, and disavowed father. Catharsis was at last permissible.

In *Counter-Attack* Sassoon paints war nearly as faithfully as he could. The poems present the ugliness of war without flinching. Sometimes bitter and sardonic, other times elegiac, the poems are those of a haunted man, certainly "a spontaneous overflow of powerful feelings" and emotion recollected not in tranquillity but in a tormented lull between terrors.

Picture-Show

Dedicated to John Masefield, *Picture-Show,* although published in Britain in 1919 and America in 1920, is primarily a war product. The writing of the poems straddled the armistice, but Sassoon could not wind down overnight. His war machine ran on, and the war themes remained in his work: death, suffering, pain, and grief. Twelve of 41 pieces are war poems. The fuller American edition contains 48 poems, including two published in *War Poems 1919*: "In an Underground Dressing Station" and "Atrocities."

The poems of *Picture-Show* continue to revolve around emotional conflict. After all, a soldier's war, unlike a civilian's or a politician's, is ultimately a personal affair. Sassoon is more and more caught by the conflict between his desire to attend with skill to his renewed duties as a company officer in combat and his moral responsibility as a "legislating poet" to warn the public of the cost and folly of the war. When relieved from battle by wounds and peace, he used his satiric skills to fight for remembrance and respect for veterans. But another initial response to demobilization was to try to return to his old, prewar ways of living and writing, a process reflected in two-thirds of the poems in *Picture-Show.*

The war poems in *Picture-Show* are the earliest work in the collection. The first written, "In an Underground Dressing Station," was composed in June 1917. The poem is a snapshot of suffering. A wounded soldier on a stretcher is screaming with pain and begging the battle surgeon to "put my leg down, doctor, do!"[16] Unbeknownst to him "He'd been shot / Horribly through the guts" (*P-S,* 10). The doctor kindly and gently comforts him, "but he was dying" (*P-S,* 10).

"Concert Party (Egyptian Base Camp)" and "Night on the Convoy (Alexandria-Marseilles)" are products of Sassoon's brief service in the Middle East early in 1918. They are descriptive poems that ask the readers to remember that soldiers, despite "uniformity," are individual, sensitive human beings moved by song. Asleep they are "prostrate and defenceless," while the persona, embarked for France once more, remembers the Battle of Arras, "Where dumb with pain I stumbled among the dead" (*P-S,* 6). Ironically, the soldiers are "going home . . . victims" (*P-S,* 6) to death.

"I Stood with the Dead," "The Dug-Out," and "Battalion Relief" are 1918 combat poems, written before Sassoon was shot in the head on 13 July. They show the officer-persona in deep depression. As implied in the first title, his living troops are doomed, but he is still mourning for the "lad that I loved" (*P-S,* 11), whom he envisions dead-eyed in the grave.

"The Dug-Out" is an eight-line masterpiece in which Sassoon, in a moderate, controlled tone, conveys "the unutterable horror of a world where nerves and imagination have been so swamped by death that the speaker can no longer bear the sight of a fellow soldier asleep" (Lane, 96–97). In trench warfare death is more common than sleep. The persona awakens a sleeping soldier, whose huddled body reminds him of a corpse. Sleep is too like death, and it saddens. In the envoi the persona thinks *"You are too young to fall asleep for ever; / And when you sleep you remind me of the dead"* (P-S, 7). Sassoon's emotive exchanges between himself and his reader are often most effective when he uses literal imagery almost exclusively. The metaphoric leap to comprehension comes from the total impression rather than from odd tropes. At its best the irony is subtle, understated, and intrinsic: in a normal world the dead look as if they are sleeping; on the battlefield the sleeping look as if they are dead.

"Battalion-Relief," like "The Dug-Out," revives the satiric animus and passion of *Counter-Attack.* A battalion is moving into the line at dusk. A battle seems to be ensuing, but no one is sure. The officer-persona thinks, "Poor blundering files, / Sweating and blindly burdened; who's to know / If death will catch them in those two dark miles?" (P-S, 9). The envoi finds the persona surprised, by gunfire, out of his meditative moment: *"What's that? . . . Oh, Sergeant-Major, don't get shot! / And tell me, have we won this war or not?"* (P-S, 9). How is anyone to know anything in that Brownian movement called war?

"Reconciliation" and "Memorial Tablet (Great War)" were written around the time of the armistice. In the former Sassoon directly and unequivocally calls on the British to remember "The German soldiers who were loyal and brave" (P-S, 2). The latter poem acerbically attacks recruiting and the class pressure employed to get men to enlist in the army. The ghost of a dead soldier watches the "Squire" who bullied him into joining the army, glancing at his name on a memorial tablet in church. But the soldier "died in hell" (P-S, 12). The poem asks sardonically, "What greater glory could a man desire?" (P-S, 12). What greater glory than to have your name on a memorial?

"Devotion to Duty," like "Aftermath," "Atrocities," and "Everyone Sang," is a postarmistice poem, part of the winding-down process for a soldier-poet. An incident that seems to be taking place in wartime Britain has the king "scan the G.H.Q. dispatch," which talks of the death in action of one of his bravest officers. The king

> gripped his beard; then closed his eyes and said,
> "Bathsheba must be warned that he is dead.
> Send for her. I will be the first to tell
> This wife how her heroic husband fell."
>
> (*P-S,* 23)

Sassoon cleverly universalizes just as he particularizes by revealing his subject to be the biblical tale of David, Uriah, and Bathsheba. Thus Sassoon commences the transition of his poetry from the specifics of war to the generalities of peace. The great irony of the poem is in its title, an irony not revealed until the last stanza. Uriah's "Devotion to Duty" has cost him his life and provided the lusting king with easy access to his widow.

"Aftermath" shows how the memory of the war lingered in the disturbed consciousness of combat veterans like Sassoon. The refrain of "Aftermath" is "Have you forgotten yet?" (*P-S,* 47). Sassoon wants the veterans to remember such events as "the dark months you held the sector at Mametz" and "The nights you watched and wired and dug and piled sandbags on parapets" (*P-S,* 47). They must "swear by the green of the spring," the symbol of their spared lives, that they will remember "corpses rotting" and dying eyes and lolling heads." Most important, they "must stop and ask: 'Is it all going to happen again?'" (*P-S,* 48). It was vital for Sassoon that the 1914–18 sacrifice not be repeated. Of course, it would be, in 1939–45.

"Atrocities" is a strident, biting attack on those veterans "Still talking big and boozing in a bar" who boast that they "butchered prisoners" (*P-S,* 13). Sassoon hated the miles gloriosus.

"Everyone Sang" is the last war poem, the "magnificent climax."[17] It is a lyrical, soldier's celebration of the arrival of peace, replete with hope and joy: "I was filled with such delight / As prisoned birds must find in freedom" (*P-S,* 56). Placed at the end of the collection, it augures an optimistic future. Sassoon later claimed that "the singing would never be done" (*P-S,* 56) "was the Social Revolution which I believed to be at hand" (*SJ,* 211), but as the revolution had not taken place and the armistice, with all its outburst of joy and happiness, had, the poem surely was a reaction to the end of the war. Sassoon also says that the poem was "essentially an expression of relief, and signified a thankfulness for liberation from the war years which came to the surface with the advent of spring" (*SJ,* 210). Although the final wish is that "the singing will never be done" (*P-S,* 56), it stopped very soon.

With exceptions, the war poems in *Picture-Show* are somewhat anticlimactic. Because of his wounds Sassoon was free of the war even before it ended. His prophetic and satiric functions were suspended. The handful of war poems here sing farewell to the red god Mars.

Many of the other poems in *Picture-Show* are love poems, physical and metaphysical. Louis Untermeyer called them "reflections of an emotion that is half-celebrated, half-stifled."[18] They are tinged with *tristesse* and are often fresh in theme if not in style.

"The Imperfect Lover" begins in the manner of John Donne with "I never asked you to be perfect—did I?" (*P-S,* 42), and concludes in the manner of Walter de la Mare, with "Then I should know, at least, that truth endured, / Though love had died of wounds" (*P-S,* 43). The promising poem ultimately disappoints as Sassoon sinks back into Pre-Raphaelite diction, as the persona states: "I'd have you stand / And look me in the eyes, and laugh, and smite me" (*P-S,* 43). The reader wants to shout, "Hit!"

"The Dark House," "Idyll," "Parted," "Lovers," "Slumber-Song," and "Vision" seem like poetic exercises, with the reader never convinced that the poems are based on any kind of actual experiences, because they are so contrived, pinched, and self-consciously symbolic.

"The Dark House" is more skillfully written and a somewhat more objective narrative than the others. A lover has visited the persona's house in the black of night, but "the house was shuttered for slumber," and so the visitor "passed the gate," but the persona hears "A quavering thrush" shrill, "Come back; come back . . . to the heart of the passion-plighted man" (*P-S,* 36). In "Idyll" the persona expects to find his lover "in the grey summer garden," where they will "share . . . Joy in the world, and peace, and dawn's one star" (*P-S,* 37). "Parted" has the persona sleepless and dreary "And in my loneliness, longing for you (*C-P,* 38). Everything he does in "this city of intense / Arteried activities . . . is but a beating down of that suspense / Which holds me from your arms" (*P-S,* 38). The sonnet "Lovers" is like the sound of old music, an ancient folk ballad or a madrigal:

> Sleep well: for I can follow you, to bless
> And lull your distant beauty where you roam;
> And with wild songs of hoarded loveliness
> Recall you to these arms that were your home.

(P-S, 40)

The sonnet "Slumber-Song" speaks of the persona's observation of his lover in bed: "Time shall be / Only slow rhythmic swaying; and your breath" (*P-S*, 41). The persona of "Visions," like Keats, loves "all things that pass" (*P-S*, 44). He cries out, "O Beauty, born of lonely things that die!" (*P-S*, 44). What succeeds in these conservative poems is their intimacy when Sassoon eschews "poetic" diction. If presented, they certainly would have flattered and moved his lovers. These poems are so different in subject and diction from the combat poems as to seem to be written by another poet.

Three poems in *Picture-Show* are about film and dance. The title poem effectively re-creates the perplexed feelings of someone seeing actual war films long after the events shown: "And still, between the shadow and the blinding flame, / The brave despair of men flings onward" (*P-S*, 1). Once reality, now art, "life is just the picture dancing on a screen" (*P-S*, 1). Sassoon cannot forget the dead whom he knew and cared for, but no coherence or insight emerges from the montage of images, representation, and memory. The meaning is that there is no meaning.

"Cinema Hero" satirizes the banal escapism and mesmerizing power of the silent film: "O, This is more than fiction! It's the truth / That somehow never happened" (*P-S*, 27). The persona, like Walter Mitty, becomes a half-dozen romantic heroes, including cowboy and cavalier, but after the movies there is ugly reality reluctantly considered: "Well what's the news to-night about the Strike?" (*P-S*, 28).

"To Leonide Massine in 'Cleopatra'" celebrates a superb ballet dancer, and the need for veterans and other civilians to leave behind the terrible and debilitating memories of the war. In deep depression the persona sees all phenomena in terms of his own dark experience. Massine, like all performing artists, is "Beauty doomed and perfect for an hour" (*P-S*, 14). Spectators

> watch you fall
> Knowing that to-morrow you will dance again.
> But not to ebbing music were they slain
> Who sleep in ruined graves, beyond recall.
>
> (*P-S*, 14)

Can beauty ever save those who have been brushed by the wingtips of despair? Can art help in forgetting?

Sassoon is trying to capture some of the confusion and suffering of the British people that is just beginning to wane. Civilian pleasures bring relief but also guilt. The war revived in film and literature tears scabs and opens wounds.

"Miracles" is a dream poem in which the persona experiences hallucinatory, Coleridgean phenomena. The dream world is full of joy and beauty but, sadly, is only a dream. On awakening he "wondered where on earth I'd been" (*P-S*, 21). "Sporting Acquaintances" and "What the Captain Said at the Point-to-Point" are humorous sports poems, the former a sonnet that parodies the difficulty in communicating with "sporting acquaintances" who are apelike in their density and lack of verbal skills; the latter, a poem that laughs at the rider who, when knocked down in steeplechasing, enjoys the pain: "Anyhow I've had a good bump round" (*P-S*, 26).

"Butterflies" and "Wraiths" are nature poems. In the first the butterfly's life of "deftly flickering over the flowers" while enjoying a brief time of "dancing through / This fiery-blossom'd revel of the hours" (*P-S*, 33) is compared to the life of the poet. In "Wraith" sound and meter win out over sense and matter in lines like "In love's night-memoried hall" (*P-S*, 34).

The persona in "To a Childless Woman" patriarchally presumes that a middle-aged woman must be suffering if she has never had a child. He sympathizes with her "Dreams of the unborn" (*P-S*, 45) as he watches her, "tender and bitter-sweet and shy . . . holding / Another's child" (*P-S*, 46), for he too has longed to have a child. "Prelude to an Unwritten Masterpiece" is a work of nostalgia and dreaming, with the persona engaging in a bit of Freudian self-analysis: "last night I dreamt an old recurring scene— / Some complex out of childhood; (sex, of course!)" (*P-S*, 51). The poet hopes someday to be able to write a long and worthwhile poem, but this is not to be it. He will become an ancient bard with a beard "drifting whiter / On bowed, prophetic shoulders" (*P-S*, 52). He mocks his own pretentiousness when he has a friend query, "Why can't you cut it short, you pompous blighter?" (*P-S*, 52). "Limitations" is also about a poet's self-critical insight: "You've got your limitations; let them sing" (*P-S*, 53). He knows that "words are fools / Who follow blindly . . . but thoughts are Kingfishers that haunt the pools / Of quiet" (*P-S*, 54). The struggle is determining what to do with his life now that the great moment of intensity and action has passed. The answer: "Go on, whoever you are" (*P-S*, 54).

"Early Chronology" begins Sassoon's healthy attempt to direct his satiric techniques, developed in the war poems, to questions and problems of postwar civilian life. A professor of archaeology is lecturing on Lydian coinage, but the moon above the trees distracts the persona, for it has "a pre-dynastic look" (*P-S,* 19). The persona, like many a student, is skeptical of the professor's erudition and his valorizing of taxonomy. The moon is art and love and life, and it beckons.

The remaining poems in *Picture-Show* are poems of remembrance. "Memory" recognizes that "death has made me wise and better and strong; / And I am rich in all that I have lost" (*P-S,* 15). But Sassoon has reverted to singing of "the darkness and the nightingale" (*P-S,* 15), and self-conscious artifice produces artificiality. "To a Very Wise Man" is a conventional poem in which Sassoon first creates a scholar whose "soul is full of cities with dead names" (*P-S,* 16), but the persona is frightened by thoughts and dreams of death. After the war he thinks, "In a strange house I woke" (*P-S,* 16). He needs consolation from the wise man: "above the years / You soar. . . . Is death so bad? . . . I wish you'd say" (*P-S,* 17). Having seen so much death, Sassoon, of course, can still not know it. There is no comfort, not even from a wise man, only the "curtained doom."

"Elegy (to Robert Ross)" is Sassoon's thank-you to his impresario, recently deceased at the time of the writing. The poem is weak, declamatory, and not evocative of Ross's life or work. Sassoon runs out of ideas, concluding with the prosaic "O heart of hearts! . . . O friend of friends" (*P-S,* 20). "The Goldsmith" is about the continuity of craftsmanship from the time of "Gnossos, in the isle of Crete" (*P-S,* 22). The sonnet "Ancient History" employs the Old Testament theme of the loss of a son. Adam, representing fathers who lost sons in the war, is presented as "a brown old vulture in the rain," while Cain is lamented as "A lion laired in the hills . . . hungry and fierce with deeds of huge desire," but Abel was "soft and fair . . . afraid to fight" (*P-S,* 24). Cain was the warrior son; Abel, the pacifist. Adam does not know if murder is more of a disgrace than Abel's cowardice, but in the end the question is moot for "the gaunt wild man whose lovely sons were dead" (*P-S,* 24). The poem works well as a parable for the moral blindness of the older generation during the war. Old men remain a major target for Sassoon.

"Fancy Dress" presents anger and the will to make war as atavistic urges. Sassoon uses Native Americans for his construct, but people throughout history have felt hate grow in their hearts even "as they knelt / Praying to gods. . . . in heavens where tomahawks are barred" (*P-S,* 29). "Middle-Ages" follows the primitive, and *"Men must be cruel and proud, / Jousting for death"* (*P-S,* 29). In "The Portrait" the persona looks at a painting from the early seventeenth century and wonders how the subject, a young man like himself, might "match [his] dreams with mine" (*P-S,* 32). "The Phantom" has yet another ghost haunting the persona, who cries, "Good angels, help me to forget" (*P-S, 35*). Last, in "Falling Asleep" someone is singing a song about a soldier, causing the persona to remember watching "the marching of my soldiers, / And count their faces; faces; sunlit faces" (*P-S, 50*). The thought, like counting sheep, allows him to sleep, with "the world / I've known; all fading past me into peace" (*P-S, 50*). This late 1919 poem is indicative of Sassoon's feelings in his time of easing posttraumatic stress. He was beginning to be able to sleep and perchance to dream without the rub.

In *Picture-Show* Sassoon rises from the bloodbath of battle to find some distraction and healing in the comforts of peace and the pleasures of life, no longer charged with terror and hate, while he commences the exorcism of the soldier-ghosts. *Picture-Show* is his passport to aftermath.

The War Poems of Siegfried Sassoon

Of the 64 poems in *The War Poems of Siegfried Sassoon*, all but one appeared first in *The Old Huntsman, Counter-Attack,* or *Picture-Show.* Sassoon and his London publisher, his friend William Heinemann, wanted to bring all the war poems together in one volume, separating out the earlier, contemplative Pre-Raphaelite and Georgian pastoral lyrics. *The War Poems of Siegfried Sassoon* and Wilfred Owen's *Poems* (1921, collected by Sassoon) are the two most important collections of war poetry to emerge from World War I.

"Return of the Heroes," written in October 1919, almost a year after the armistice, is a satiric monologue in which a "lady" in a crowd is watching a victory parade. She is blissfully unaware of the sacrifices the common soldiers have made, as her eyes can see only the leaders and the rows of ribbons on their tunics. At the head is "Sir Henry Dudster! Such a splendid leader!"[19] The marshals and the generals were all duds to Sassoon. The "lady" thinks that the "heroes" must feel sad because they cannot win any more victories. Once more Sassoon's animadversion to women is shown, implying that they are scatterbrained, shallow, and completely unaware of the cost of a war that took the lives of so many of their husbands, sons, and brothers.

In 1983 Rupert Hart-Davis collected, arranged, and dated all of *The War Poems of Siegfried Sassoon.*[20] Of the 113 poems included, 13 survived in manuscripts and journals, and 7 had appeared only in periodicals.

Sassoon's war poetry encompasses many modes: satiric, elegiac, comic, horrific, shocking, vengeful, and even pastoral. The poems were extremely therapeutic for himself and his readers, both civilian and military. For Sassoon and his comrades in arms, poetry, both the writing and the reading of it, gave a little dignity to the existential insult of their experiences, and it helped rationalize the bomb bursts of emotion, fear, terror, dehumanization, and horror that, understandably, could lead to insanity. For civilians the poetry permitted guilt and masochistic self-punishment as a way of sharing the suffering and trying to atone for what they had inflicted on their own young.

Sassoon's war poetry is direct and effective, with clear, hard, tough, epigrammatic, literal language and a minimum of metaphor. The poems are minidramas and tableaux. Wisely Sassoon "remained aware of his limitations and did not attempt a profundity that was beyond him: his gifts were pre-eminently those of a satirist, and it was in satire that he excelled" (Bergonzi, 105). Sassoon's syntax marks time, allowing irony its breakthrough. He is at his best when he combines pity for Tommy's ordeal with indignation at the mindlessness and cruelty of the war, the stupidity of the generals and their staffs, and the contemptible vapidity of civilians who closed their eyes to the slaughter in France. The major binaries of Sassoon's world at war are civilians/soldiers, staff/fighters, and old/young, but not friend/foe or German/English. Sassoon's poetry "performed the great service of debunking the old romantic myth of the glory of war" (Pinto, 145). The war poets in toto related experience to brutal reality as it had never been done before. Sassoon's literary influence as the modern creator of the language of war continues, while his moral authority has guided men and women in the "war over war" ever since. A small body of verse effected this: "It is by virtue of thirty or forty poems that delineate the agony of the fighting in the trenches that he holds an honoured place among English poets" (Press, 46).

Perhaps finally, the appreciation for Sassoon, as with Owen, is in the pity of it all.

Chapter Four

"An Art to Resurrect the Rose"

Later Poems

Siegfried Sassoon strongly resented that the world had changed with the advent of World War I. He hated "progress" as the twentieth century defined it: "I must confess that I have no desire to travel five hundred miles in a minute, or to scrutinize the Prime Minister of Ruritania on a television screen. Unsuited by temperament to unlimited mobility of mind and body, I am no enthusiast for the conquest of space. Let me add that I have always entertained a positive personal antipathy to the universe. It is too much for me, and that is all I can say about it."[1] Clearly the century disappointed and disillusioned Sassoon.

Sassoon's imagination remained primarily fixed on his 1914–18 experiences. B. Ifor Evans states that "nothing . . . happened later that could be admitted into the intimate places of his mind."[2] Sassoon's wartime rage had passed like a fierce storm, leaving only a slightly rippled sea. Without anger he was without energy. His poetry moved from social satire to modest, gentle, self-effacing, pacifism, and later religious verse. Sassoon's post–World War I poems show little motion or growth. They are generally muted, diffident, absentious, and colorless. Yet they employ a Wordsworthian directness, a sharp focus, and a renewed, vitalizing interest in and love for nature. Sassoon now seldom resorts to shock, and uses the epigrammatic technique and colloquial language less frequently. There is "evident growth in control" (Maguire, 124), as Sassoon's poetic art cooled and became more careful and precise. Last, God is rehabilitated.

As before the war, Sassoon often published individual poems or small collections privately and in limited editions. As a postwar poet he adopted two roles: peace prophet, employing satire to expose corruption, greed, and social injustice in society and to deter humankind's predilection for conflict; and after 1940, religious recluse tending his soul.

62

Satirical Poems

The need to understand the causes of the war and to place blame provoked a burst of satire in the 1920s, particularly in the work of Osbert Sitwell, Humbert Wolfe, and Siegfried Sassoon.[3] After republishing for the trade 67 poems from *The Old Huntsman, Counter-Attack,* and *Picture-Show* in *Selected Poems* (1925), and 32 poems in *Augustan Book* (1926), all but 2 of which had been previously published, Sassoon's next trade collection was *Satirical Poems* (1926), containing 32 poems, all but 6 of which had been privately published in *Recreations* (1923) and *Lingual Exercises* (1925). "Sporting Acquaintances" and "Early Chronology" came from *Picture-Show*; "On Reading the War Diary of a Defunct Ambassador," from *Augustan Book*. The new poems are "Monday on the Demolition of Devonshire House," "Lines Written in Anticipation of a London Paper Attaining a Guaranteed Circulation of Ten Million Daily," and "On Some Portraits by Sargent." The 1933 edition contains 5 additional poems: "The Utopian Times," "Mammoniac Ode," "Memorial Service for an Honest Soldier," "The Traveller to His Soul," and "The Facts."

Satirical Poems contains most of Sassoon's postwar satires, chastising politicians, women, the press, academics, the rich, and the aristocracy. Simultaneously he begins the idealization of Edwardian and late Victorian times that culminates in the autobiographies, *The Old Century and Seven Years More* and the *Weald of Youth.* Sassoon seldom wrote about the disadvantaged, and *Satirical Poems* contains most of his few emotional, socialist statements. Although satirized, the wealthy are Sassoon's most frequent subject, next to himself. He felt for the underdogs; he ran with the top dogs. Of Sassoon's satiric writings, Bergonzi notes: "Throughout the twenties, when he continues to have left-wing leanings, Sassoon wrote sharp, epigrammatic verses that sniped at authority and conventional attitudes. In this respect he was at one with his age" (Bergonzi, 107). Against instinct and inclination Sassoon tries hard to remain contemporary in *Satirical Poems,* depicting such immediate events as a college founder's feast day, evensong at Westminster Abbey, a Stravinsky concert, and a dinner in a restaurant on Fifth Avenue. Onto these events he grafts his indignation and dissatisfaction.

The now-urbane civilian Sassoon satirizes a former ambassador in "On Reading the War Diary of a Defunct Ambassador." Serving the Foreign Office during the war, the only guns the ambassador knew were for "peppering partridges, grouse, or pheasant."[4] The poet is glad the ambassador has exposed his "visionless officialized fatuity." Sassoon excoriates the diplomat: "The world will find no pity in your pages; / No exercise of spirit worthy of mention" (SP, 12). In "Monday on the Demolition of Devonshire House" Sassoon laments the loss of historical buildings where great persons, like the poet Byron, once lived or visited. Sassoon attacks the rich, who care for nothing but newness, wealth, and pleasure, but also derides "Myself, whose arrogance is mostly brainy" (SP, 12). "Lines Written in Anticipation of a London Paper Attaining a Guaranteed Circulation of Ten Million Copies," Sassoon's longest title, takes a shot at the media and mass culture, ending with a malediction: "I damn your Circulation as a whole, / And leave you to your twice-ten-million readers" (SP, 16).

In "The Grand Hotel" Sassoon humorously attacks manifestations of materialism: "Resolved to satirize Hotels-de-Luxe, / Shyly I sift the noodles from the crooks" (SP, 17), while in "Breach of Decorum" the poet cleverly rips social affectation as he describes a society matron, "Lady Luce": "I have observed her evening-party eyes." She collects and patronizes celebrities, but to her dismay the persona's "intellectual gloom encroached / Upon the scintillance of champagne chatter" (SP, 19). The annual Oxford-Cambridge cricket match is made fun of with eighteenth-century closed couplets in "The Blues of Lords":

> My intellectual feet approach this function
> With tolerance and Public-School compunction;
> Aware that, whichsoever side bats best,
> their partisans are equally well-dressed.
>
> (SP, 22)

It is regrettable that Sassoon did not employ this satiric, juxtapositional verse form more often.

The persona in "Reynardism Revisited," a fox-hunter, has friends, the "Fernie-Goldflakes," who think him to be mad and "an anachronism" (SP, 24). But he, "Refortified by exercise and air," grows "half-humane" and questions the propriety of his "sport."

"The Case for Miners" is Sassoon's one true socialist poem in *Satirical Poems* and the most effective piece in the collection. Upper-class diners, "peeling their plover eggs," attack the persona for defending the working class and the striking miners. After all, "Why should a miner earn six pounds a week? / Leisure! They'd only spend it in a bar!" (SP, 21). The "port-flushed" rich would almost like to see the strikers "hawking matches in the gutter" (*SP,* 21). Plutocracy shows its ugliest face in this satire worthy of the author of *Counter-Attack.*

"Founder's Feast," a satire on Oxford, also comes close to Sassoon at war. The university, as part of the establishment, has colluded in the destruction of a generation of its own product. It deserves his asperity. A "toothless Regius Professor / Ebbed the Madeira wine" (*SP,* 55) as the graduates drink the health of "Edward the Confessor," and honor the guest, "great Major-General Bluff. . . . Enough, enough, enough, enough, enough!" (*SP,* 55). Sassoon is ready to scream at the old, smug murderers in red-tabbed khaki. On the other hand, Oxford is a place of peace and beauty, where, as in "Sheldonian Soliloquy (during Bach's B Minor Mass)" the persona hears "song that from ecclesiasmus cries / Eternal *Resurrexit* to the living" (*SP,* 56).

"Nature-loving ladies" in "An Old-World Effect" paint rustic thatch-roofed cottages instead of "a Cubist housing-scheme" (*SP,* 38). They portray the past instead of providing for the future. Sassoon takes on the battered British Empire and Kipling's "Recessional" in "Afterthoughts on the Opening of the British Empire Exhibition." In rolling anapests and alliterations the persona "listened and stared," only "one face in a stabilized flock," at busbies, bayonets, and "golden drum-majors," all the "Ebullitions of Empire exulted." It is all "Patriotic paradings with pygmy preciseness" despite music by Elgar and lyrics by Blake (*SP,* 9).

"Villa D'Este Gardens," "Fantasia on a Wittelsbach Atmosphere," "Memorandum," "A Stately Exterior," "Observations in Hyde Park," and "Storm on Fifth Avenue" gently ridicule internationalism, modernity, and the postwar international good life in the haunts of the rich: "O Babylon! O Carthage! O New York!" (*SP,* 30). Despite satires like "The Case for the Miners" and "Breach of Decorum," Sassoon was trying to escape his time. The travel and "stately homes and gardens" poems are peopled with the likes of Byron, Tennyson, the duke of Marlborough, admirals, generals, "painted ladies," and "William, Victoria, Edward" (*SP,* 34). Like so many British living beyond the watershed of World War I, Sassoon ached for the past, as does the girl in "Observations in Hyde Park," listening to a "scarlet band. . . . that thrilled flounced-muslin maidenhood to tears; / The horses snort; she sighs for vanished lords" (*SP,* 27).

The remaining new poems in *Satirical Poems* are devoted to cultural subjects: visual art and its museums, music, and theater. "In the National Gallery" is a sonnet attacking jaded museum patrons with "Unspeculative faces, bored and weak" (*SP,* 39). "The London Museum" takes on antiquarians, who are content to fill "their noses / With aromatic dust of some episode in History" (*SP*, 40). Sassoon pities them for their "aversion from the flowing vistas of the Future!" (*SP*, 40). "In the Turner Rooms (at the Tate Gallery)" shows the persona's confusion over his love of art and the demands of life. A "calm student with . . . red-brown hair" distracts him from the brilliant canvases. After all, "That young head / Is life, the unending challenge . . . Turner's dead" (*SP*, 42). "On Some Portraits by Sargent" deplores the painter's commercialism, for which he "ladies lovelified to ball-room pitch" (*SP*, 44). Social affectation has a bold nemesis in Sassoon.

Again in "Evensong in Westminster Abbey" the persona finds it hard to concentrate on genius like "the illustrious Dead" around him in the abbey, because "Dogma has sent Antiquity to sleep / With sacrosant stultiloquential drone" (*SP*, 46). Sassoon's verse here is itself "stultiloquential." The sonnet "Hommage à Mendelssohn" pronounces the composer's music able to "charm us and assuage / With amiable concinnity of style" (*SP*, 52), "the sinking chords" welcome "for what they're worth" (*SP*, 52), whereas Stravinsky in "Concert-Interpretation (Le Sacre du Printemps)" deeply moves the persona: "savagery pervades Me" (*SP*, 54). Stravinsky's "April" can "Incendiarize the Hall with resinous fires" (*SP*, 54). As a summation, "A Musical Critic Anticipates Eternity" and finds it not quite the composition it could be. He expects to critique creation thus: "The music was devoid of all divinity!" (*SP*, 51).

"First Night: *Richard III*" finds the persona admiring Shakespeare's great villain. "A Post-Elizabethan Tragedy" petulantly attacks the audience, a "crowd / Of intellectual fogies, fools, and freaks" (*SP*, 49) at a performance of John Ford's *'Tis Pity She's a Whore.*

"Solar Eclipse," the last poem in the 1926 *Satirical Poems*, is a classical piece relating the legend of the unsuccessful pursuit by Apollo of the goddess Daphne, whose "green shadowed flesh / Writhes arborescent" (*SP*, 61). The poem is artificial, contrived, and completely out of place in a collection of poems on contemporary subjects and themes.

"The Utopian Times" in the 1933 *Satirical Poems* describes a "newspaper" published only once a year that stands for the failure of achieved socialism. Information is totally controlled and always "cheerful," for "no credible report / has reached us, in twelve months, of any 'crimes.'"[5] In only five years Sassoon had turned his back on socialism. "Mammoniac Ode," written on 30 September 1931 in the depth of the Great Depression, attacks international banking in a satiric, hymnlike lyric, ending with the prayer "Deliver us, O Lord, from Currency Inflation" (*SP33*, 65).

Set in Westminster Abbey, "Memorial Service for an Honest Soldier" attacks the establishment at the event: ambassadors, clergy, lawyers, and the silk-hat crowd, all unworthy of the soldier, "An incorruptible persistent man" (*SP33,* 66). "The Traveller to His Soul" and "The Facts" are not satires. The former is a precursor of *The Heart's Journey* and Sassoon's subsequent spiritual verse. He states the great question of the last half of his life: "That problem which concerns me most—about / Which I have entertained the gravest doubt— / Is, bluntly stated, 'Have I got a soul?'" (*SP33,* 68). "The Facts" of life are "fierce" and hard to face, for the twentieth century has exposed "the jungle" that is "within us" (*SP33,* 69).

Sassoon set a noble task for himself in *Satirical Poems*: to expose and attack venality and vice, as well as hypocrites and humbugs, memorialists and mammonists. For the most part he failed. His heart wasn't in it. With death for himself and those he loved no longer imminent, he could no longer hate. Sassoon had become "too pensive and withdrawn a spirit for the service of this blunt drill-sergeant art."[6]

The Heart's Journey

First published in a 1927 limited edition, *The Heart's Journey* contains 35 poems in the enlarged 1928 ordinary edition. Several of the poems had been previously published in such private editions as *Lingual Exercises for Advanced Vocabularians* (1925) and single-poem printings. Two poems, "Lovers" and "Elegy (to R.R.)," were reprinted from *Picture-Show.* Sassoon gave the collection its title because he had decided to place his recent "love and lyrical poems" in it.[7] In a sense *Satirical Poems* is Sassoon's *Songs of Experience* and *The Heart's Journey* his *Songs of Innocence. The Heart's Journey* is an attempt to effect a surcease of psychological pain by means of concentration on romantic imagery and Pre-Raphaelite sentiments, as evinced in the invocation (1): "Soul, be my song; return arrayed in white; / Lead home the loves that I have wronged and slain; / Bring back the summer dawns that banished night."[8]

Thus in *The Heart's Journey* Sassoon begins his long spiritual journey, the search for the essence of selfhood and the soul. His method, modeled after the seventeenth-century metaphysical poets, is to examine his own heart and write spiritual autobiography, as in the contemplative sonnet 25, "At the Grave of Henry Vaughan," in which he expresses a desire to meld selfhood with his favorite metaphysical poet: "Here sleeps the Silurist; the loved physician . . . here faith and mercy, wisdom and humility . . . shine"

(*HJ,* 33), and the persona stands by the grave, "a suppliant at the door" (*HJ,* 33).

The poems 2, "Sing bravely my heart..."; 3, "As I was walking in the gardens..."; 4, "What you are I cannot say..."; 5, "You were glad tonight..." (from *Picture-Show*); 6, "While I seek you..."; 7, "Now when we two have been apart..."; and 11, "Farewell to a Room," are short, delicate, cryptic love poems of "night-long thought" (*HJ,* 12), "confederate silences" (*HJ,* 17), and the "Paradise" of passion.

The poems 8, "In me, past, present, future meet..."; 9, "Since thought is life..."; and 13, "In the stars..."; and the sonnets 26, "A Midnight Interior"; 27, "One Who Watches"; 28, "It has been told..."; 29, "I cannot pray..."; 32, "The wisdom of the world..."; and 35, "A Last Judgment," are religio-philosophical poems calling on beneficient spirits for "strength to find / From lamp and flower simplicity of mind" (*HJ,* 34). Sexual demons are banished in favor of chaste angels. Acceptance of fate is made central for happiness, and the loss of love is feared more than the end of life.

Music poems include 15, "When Selfhood can discern...," in which the persona sings prosaically of the timelessness and healing power of "Beethoven, Bach, Mozart" (*HJ,* 21), and 24, "From a Fugue by Bach," in which musical notes bring "voices from vastness divine" (*HJ,* 32) that make life livable. The poem 19, "To an Eighteenth Century Poet," also extols the immortality of great artists: "Who then shall dare to say that they have died?" (*HJ,* 25).

The sonnet 14, "Strangeness of Heart," lauds the renewing quality of nature and the need of the persona to keep the "simple spells" (*HJ,* 20) that stir childhood. A "garden bird who sang / Strangeness of heart" (*HJ,* 20) may be Sassoon's coded indication of his sexual preference. It came from nature and evolved in childhood. In the sonnet 18, "Alone, I hear the wind...," the wind brings "the last flower / From gardens where I'll nevermore return" (*HJ,* 24). City life creates a longing for the pleasures of gardens and the "earliest ecstasies."

The poem 22, "To One Who Was with Me in the War," is the most poignant and moving poem in *The Heart's Journey*. The persona daydreams about going up the line to battle one night, 10 years earlier, in the war, in the company of a friend. The fear and horror are relived. Now the friend has grown older, of course. The persona remembers "how you looked,—your ten-years-vanished face, / Hoping the War will end next week" (*HJ,* 30). In the end the persona is snapped out of his love-hate reverie. The sonnet 23, "On Passing the New Menin Gate," is also a postwar "war" poem. Sassoon is trying to end the game of ghosts. It is almost "Sassoon's last word on the War" (Thorpe, 37), written in an angry, bitter mode. The memorial gate at Ypres proclaims the immortality of the war dead, but Sassoon sardonically remarks, "Well might the Dead who struggled in the slime / Rise and deride this sepulchre of crime" (*HJ*, 31).

Near the end of the collection the poems 30, "All Souls' Day," and 31, "The Power and the Glory," affirm a positive faith in the life force. That "faith, absolved from fear, / Sings out into the morning" (*HJ*, 38), and thus ghosts are dispelled through holy thought. The persona exclaims, "*Let there be life,* said God. . . . *Let there be God,* say I. . . . *Let life be God*" (*HJ*, 39). The next-to-the-last poem in *The Heart's Journey,* 34, "A flower has opened in my heart . . . ," summarizes Sassoon's feeling and philosophy as his psyche emerges from postwar depression and disappointment. The world's secret is "the peace that shines apart," for peace brings the "Heart's miracle of inward light" (*HJ*, 43).

In *The Heart's Journey* Sassoon exhibits growing release from the specter of ghosts and the sound of guns. The search for self is well under way. Love for the living stirs him more than remembrance of the dead. Inner peace is nearer, and the heart is lightened.

Poems by Pinchbeck Lyre

In 1931 Sassoon thought it would be amusing and interesting to publish pseudonymously a collection of 14 new, mainly satiric poems. Some of the jeu d'esprit pieces parody poems by the satirist Humbert Wolfe. The book's epigram sets the tone: "It is the season of larks." Beauty and love, Sassoon's stock-in-trade in *The Heart's Journey,* are made fun of, and the poet turns up the modernity-bashing.

The language of *Poems* is often obtuse and strained, and Sassoon is self-deprecatory. In the invocating "Exordium" he begs his muse, self-mockingly, "Grant me once more my share of *succès fou.*"9 In "Conundrum" the persona-poet is still "grinding my incorrigible old organ" (*PPL*, 13), yet the lure of "Chanson Perpetuelle" causes him to be chary of "betraying the logarithm of the rose" (*PPL*, 10), for, as in "Largesse," the poem itself "unpetals its effortless / Gold idea" (*PPL*, 11).

"Écossaise" ("Scottish") is a song of praise for Scotland, where the persona would like to play the "primrose role of the Young Pretender" (*PPL*, 12). "Post-Mortem" is a maudlin sonnet, telling a lover, "If I should die you must not let it matter. / The cocktail of your tears will soon be shaken" (*PPL,* 14). In "An Alpine Horoscope" Switzerland's "eternal peaks untarnished / Mock and applaud my ever-upward yodel" (*PPL,* 15). Self-mockery continues in "Anticlimax," in which the pursuit of "Avalon" is absurd, only provoking "roars of laughter" (*PPL,* 18). Sassoon's "Cri De Coeur" ("Cry from the Heart") is that "the critics wallop / The stuff one writes" (*PPL,* 19). In "Requiem" the persona sardonically advises himself, "Swing tripe, swing tosh!" (*PPL,* 21). That is all he needs to do to "no longer worry / About your sales" (*PPL,* 21). "Coda" laments the closing of a bar, "The Cat and the Fiddle," as well as the death of the red-nosed men and women who "boozed" and now sleep (*PPL,* 20). "Chanson Gazeuse" is a paean to gas as energy, and "Will There Be Ever?" absurdly envisions a poet's paradise as a place where critics "ring euphonious / clarions" for everything composed (*PPL,* 16). Finally, "Sepulchral Epigram (from the Greek)" has the persona admit that he joined "Fleet Street" for "gain" and "my fate was rather frightful" (*PPL,* 22).

Poems by Pinchbeck Lyre, quite rightly, was not well received, and when Sassoon's authorship was ascertained, it did not enhance his reputation. But then, he did not expect it to.

The Road to Ruin

In 1932 the General Disarmament Conference failed, and pacifists despaired. Adolf Hitler came to power in 1933, the year of the publication of *The Road to Ruin,* in which Sassoon, in his 1930s role as pacifist, "predicted death by fire, gas, and disease. He offered no hope for mankind" (Cohen, 177). Sassoon is full of Old Testament pessimism. He holds up the placard of doom. Humankind has fallen.

The Road to Ruin contains seven interrelated poems of warning about "this disastrous decade." Sassoon is "like one in purgatory" having "learned the loss of hope."[10] "At the Cenotaph" he muses that "War is purgatory / Proof of the pride and power of being alive" (*RR,* 13). Sassoon believes that "The Prince of Darkness" hopes God will make humankind forget what the memorial means, the suffering of World War I. "Mimic Warfare" satirizes the pleasure some take in war "games," when "Genial tanks go grinding" (*RR,* 15). "A Premonition" has the persona, "A gas-proofed ghost," warning on chemical warfare and envisioning corpses "hunched and twisted in the stilled / Disaster of Trafalgar Square" (*RR,* 17). Hatred of war again brings out the clear, direct communicator in Sassoon.

"The Ultimate Atrocity" is the use of biological weapons, "the first bacterial bomb" (*RR,* 19). "The News from the War-after-Next" is that, as in H. G. Wells and Huxley, Britain's fate is to be a brutal nation when "the last Idealist was lynched in the morning" (*RR,* 21). In "An Unveiling" an American president is lamenting the death of London: "Not vainly London's War-gassed victim perished" (*RR,* 23). The prophet came close.

The Road to Ruin still has power to move the conscience against war. The small collection contributed to the waning but historically misguided pacifist movement in the 1930s. Sassoon, of course, underwent a change of heart in World War II.

Vigils

Published in 1935, *Vigils* contains 35 new poems, 13 more than appeared in the 1924 limited private edition. The poems are mainly austere, moody, resigned meditations. Nature-loving and ghosts abound. Protest is scant, and the romantic exuberance of *The Heart's Journey* has vanished. The nearly 50-year-old poet, no longer mordacious, has found that the world had failed to change spiritually after the suffering and sacrifice of the war, and so weltschmerz has set in. The only anodyne is truth in poetry. In searching for the true self, the heart and mind are uncertain of direction (Thorpe, 214).

The title poem, "Vigils," is the most hopeful piece. The persona stands his lonely vigil. He keeps "In a land asleep / One light burning till break of day,"[11] hoping to find "Peace, remote in the morning star" (*V,* 2). In "An Emblem" the poet, Shelley's legislator again, must "plant your tree" so that people may see "Beauty greenly growing" and "divine / Freedom bravely blowing" (*V,* 1). In "Elected Silence" the persona admits that his "heart / Translates instinctive tragic-tone" (*V,* 3).

"Vigil in Spring" and "December Stillness" have nature teaching "growth's annunciate thrust and thrill" (*V,* 4) and how "to travel far and bear my loads" (*V,* 5). Four untitled poems, referring to childhood, proclaim that "the love of life is my religion still" (*V,* 6). Childhood dreams have returned to the persona in middle age. He is glad: "They were my firstling friends" (*V,* 7). Childhood escapes on tiptoe "Down the glimmering staircase, past the pensive clock" (*V,* 8). Finally, many of the persona's earlier "selves—once proud, once passionate with young prayers" (*V,* 9)—are dead. Alas, as in "Farewell to Youth" "the dreamer that was

Youth lies dead" (V, 12), while in "Long Ago" the older, long-wandering self is "laden / Head and heart with your years" (V, 13).

In the untitled "At the end of all wrong roads ..." nature has provided strength for the journey of life, and at the end of the "wrong roads" are the "gates of the garden without a name" (V, 14), perhaps death. "War Experience" is a memory poem in which the persona, who in youth had learned the trade of war, states that "twelve winters later" hate has been purged; only the faint echo of a Somme bombardment "softly booms" (V, 15). "Ex-Service" also records the persona's fading dream of battle and the dimming memory of his dead friends: "the darkness of their dying / Grows one with War recorded" (V, 16). Some bitterness remains: *"Our deeds with lies were lauded, / Our bones with wrongs rewarded"* (V, 16).

The untitled "Break silence ..." has the sleepless persona still haunted by the past, "in that garret of uneasy gloom / Which is your brain" (V, 17), and in "We Shall Not All Sleep" the ghosts, "haunting familiar friends" (V, 19), have a beneficial effect, in that they may lead the persona and others to belief and faith and to understand "The Gains of Good" through "darkness denied" (V, 18). In the untitled "Again the dead ..." they are once more "demanding / To be," while the persona wonders if he can "empower your quiet returning" (V, 22) by living for them.

In "Revisitation," Sassoon's elegy for his deceased friend and psychiatrist, Dr. W. H. R. Rivers, the good doctor's ghost exercises "influence undiminished," while the poet is "powerless to repay" the beneficence (V, 23). The spirits in "Vibrations" bequeath experience, and in "Words for the Wordless" they are "imagined angels" whom the persona wishes alive again (V, 21).

"The Merciful Knight," although he "sleeps in stone," knows the value of mercy in a world where violent men "Rode darkly out to die" (V, 24). In "Memorandum" the "Sleeper" is powerless "in imprisoning night / To waken from a purgatorial dream" (V, 25). Sassoon's bad dreams endure as the memories of World War I are still with him, though fading, and the fears of a World War II are gestating. "Human Histories" of the dead, "like books unread," still exist "somewhere in the library of Time" (V, 26).

In the untitled "The mind of man ..." hope emerges from the "World undiscovered within us" (V, 30), whereas places where power was worshiped and idolatry thrived, like "Babylon," are "Nothing now" but "Auguries of self-annihilation" (V, 27). Thus, "Everyman" must avoid "the impassioned pigmy fist / Clenched cloudward and defiant" (V, 29), for the earth continually reminds us of our fate, as in "Ultimatum," wherein one sees "foam's oblivion whitening under crumbling coasts"

(*V,* 33) and Sassoon reminds us of the stoicism of Matthew Arnold's "Dover Beach."

Heaven is much on Sassoon's mind in *Vigils.* It is depicted in "Heaven" as "designed by man's death-fearing mind / To hallow his carnal heritage with healing" (*V,* 31) and accessible only through suffering, "the reward of racked renunciation" (*V,* 31). In "Credo" the persona waits for Heaven, although he feels unworthy and "brutish" (*V,* 32). Ghosts mark the way to Heaven in "Presences Perfected," and the great dead each triumphed "Through spirit alone" (*V,* 34). Time is the key to all mysteries. "The Hour-Glass" speaks to the persona: "I am the emblem of your phantom yesterday" (*V,* 28).

The final poem in *Vigils* is "Ode," in which the persona states that humankind has constructed the City of God from its own needs and desires. The end note of *Vigils* is pessimistic; the soul cannot "outdistance Death" (*V,* 35). Man cannot expect that "through hope shall his faults be healed" (*V,* 35).

Sassoon has escaped in *Vigils* into Henry Vaughan–like metaphysical speculations and a search for "soulhood." His mood is mainly dejected. He is resigned to living between life and death, unsure of the meaning of either, and between peace and war, unsure of the way of the world.

Rhymed Ruminations

Dedicated to Edmund Blunden and published in 1939 in a limited edition and in 1940 in an enlarged ordinary edition, the full *Rhymed Ruminations* contains 42 new poems. Stephen Spender called the collection "the best music that [Sassoon] has constructed since the war," but Spender also goes on to say that Sassoon has built "a wonderful shell around himself to protect him from the world; a shell pearled with music, painting, reading, landscape, parenthood, money."[12] Indeed the collection seems somewhat self-tranquilizing.

Except for two poems dealing with Britain at war again, "The English Spirit," composed on 19 May 1940, and "Silent Service," written on 23 May 1940, *Rhymed Ruminations* breaks no new ground for Sassoon but essentially polishes old themes. Some pieces have a Hardyesque and even a Yeatsean flavor. In "Brevities" the persona, as in an epitaph, states, "I am that man who, having lived his day, / Looks once on life and goes his wordless way."[13]

"Property" shows the persona's recognition of the temporariness of possession, as does "Outlived by Trees," in which long-lived trees "The transcience of this lifetime teach" (*RhR,* 16). Pantheistic consolation is sought through merging with nature: "And in your greenery while you last, / I shall survive who shared your past" (*RbR*, 16). "Eulogy of My House" and the nostalgic "In Heytesbury Wood" evince Sassoon's love for his estate as he remembers the previous owner and "the prosperous prime / Of your well-ordered distant mid-Victorian time" (*RbR*, 18).

"Prehistoric Burial," "A Remembered Queen," "Antiquities," "While Reading a Ghost Story," "On Edington Hill," and "878–1935" are poems recalling the secrets of old houses and the great history that weighs on English land from the earliest human inhabitation onward. "A Local Train of Thought" has the poet-persona remark that a passing night train, "the one-fifty," comforts him in its regularity, as do all things and places reliable and unchanging.

War clouds are gathering, and "A View of Old Exeter" reminds Sassoon of "That simpler world from which we've been evicted" (*RbR*, 29). "Metamorphosis" assures that reading Ovid still gives pleasure. The past rolls on like the waves of the sea. "Ideologies" satirizes human "progress," as ideas first expressed "long ago in liveliest monkey-language" have created only "Babels" (*RbR*, 32). The persona aches for the days of his youth. "Two Old Ladies" light his memory mirror in the autumn dusk" (*RbR*, 33).

"Blunden's Beech," named by Sassoon for his friend, helps him to dwell on poetry "and bring / To summer's idyll an unheeding grace" (*RbR*, 34). "November Dusk" also speaks of local pleasures: "I've no need to travel far to find / This bird who from the leafless walnut tree / Sings like the world's farewell to sight and sound" (*RbR*, 35). Sassoon is beginning to leave the cosmopolitan world in his wake. In "Wealth of Awareness," "Acceptance," "Eyes," and "Heart and Soul" the persona accepts the biological imperative called aging but insists that "Growing older, the heart's not colder: / Losing youngness, the eyes seem clearer" (before cataracts), and he recalls the "Weald of youth" (*RbR*, 38).

"A Picture of the Muse," "Tragitones," and "Midsummer Eve" are short, nostalgic pieces of remorse, guilt, and grieving for "Time, you timeless old mower of all that we men love most" (*RbR*, 41), reminding one of Ralph Hodgson's "Time, You Old Gypsy Man."

"Old World to New" asks the future to "forgive me what I lack" (*RbR*, 42). "Earth and Heaven" and "Gloria Mundi" argue that if there is a heaven it is "about me everywhere / In love's good deeds" (*RbR*, 44), while "time's tales are as light that fails" (*RbR*, 45), when the eternity that is nature reveals itself. "Silly Sooth" informs the reader that he or she must "not deny your dreams" but must find "What world within you lies" (*RhR*, 51). As for the persona, "Old Music" has over the years given peace and made for "calm content" (*RhR*, 52).

Five poems in *Rhymed Ruminations* are addressed to Sassoon's young son, George, born in 1936. Although patently sincere, they are a bit squirmy. In "Meeting and Parting" the persona is "My self reborn" when "Alone I stand before my new-born son" (*RhR*, 46). The poet begs the infant, "When I am dying and all is done, / Look on my face and say that you forgive" (*RhR*, 46). "To My Son" and "A Blessing" read like words of Polonius to Laertes. "The Child in the Window" is a well-crafted poem that finds the persona gratified that the nearly four-year-old child in the "nursery world" is unaware that "The world one map of wastening war unrolled" (*RhR*, 49). Yet the child set his "spirit free" from thought of conflict. "Progressions" then recounts for the child the ages of man yet to come, until he achieves as if in nirvana "A mind, renouncing hopes and finding lost loves holy" (*RhR*, 50).

"Thoughts in 1932" could easily have been included in *The Road to Ruin*, for it laments "The Black Thirties" and predicts that while "airmen, with high-minded motives fight / To save Futurity," in years to come panic-stricken hordes will hear the hum of warplanes "And Fear will be synonymous with Flight" (*RhR*, 14). "Silver Jubilee Celebration" brings back the ironic tone with which Sassoon attacked war in the 1915–18 poems, but now, in light of Germany's revived militarism, he has reversed his position, warning against the rise of fascism: "we must now re-educate our youth / With 'Arm or perish'" (*RhR*, 22). Sassoon portrays a new truth that he would "stitch across each Union Jack unfurled / 'No bargain struck with Potsdam is put over / Unless well backed by bombers—and Jehovah!'" (*RhR*, 23). "A Prayer from 1936" recognizes "Our need of guns" and asks the "heaven of music to absolve us from this hell" (*RhR*, 43). In "Doggerel about Old Days" Sassoon laments that "In 1909 the future was a thing desired," but "Will someone tell me where I am—in '39?" (*RhR*, 53).

"The English Spirit" calls on the courageous ghosts "who have wrought our English past / to stand near us now . . . till we have braved and broken and overcast / The cultural crusade of Teuton tanks" (*RhR*, 54). The sentiment is admirable, but the verse is dreadful. "Silent Service," remarks Joseph Cohen," is so unlike the poems which made Sassoon famous that it is difficult to accept the fact that he composed these lines" (Cohen, 178): "None are exempt from service in this hour; / And vanquished in ourselves we dare not be" (*RhR*, 55). Sassoon now believes, devoutly, that God and heaven are on the side of the Allies in World War

II, that there is such a thing as a good war, and that there are values truly worth dying for: "In every separate soul let courage shine— / A kneeling angel holding faith's front-line" (*RhR*, 55). It is as if the ghost of Rupert Brooke had entered the body of Siegfried Sassoon.

Rhymed Ruminations is a Janus of a book, looking back to Victorian and Edwardian times and reluctantly forward to a world near the apocalypse. Sassoon's thoughts and values have evolved, and in a political sense even reversed, but still he remains true to caring and concern, to sensitivity, and to a love for the natural world.

Poems Newly Selected 1916–1935 and Collected Poems

In 1940 Sassoon published a collection of 58 poems from *Selected Poems, Satirical Poems, The Heart's Journey,* and *Vigils,* entitled *Poems Newly Selected 1916–1935.* No new poems were included.

Collected Poems, published in 1947, is massive, containing 299 pieces from *The Old Huntsman, Counter-Attack, Picture-Show, Satirical Poems, The Heart's Journey, The Road to Ruin, Vigils,* and *Rhymed Ruminations.* Sassoon re-collected his poetry in 1961. *Collected Poems 1908–1956* contains 361 pieces; the additional poems are from *Sequences* (1956). *Collected Poems 1908–1956* is Sassoon's verse monument. Sassoon was as courageous in print as he was in war. He was not afraid to publish almost all of his life's work, strong and weak. Let the reader choose and decide.

In 1947 the *Times Literary Supplement,* reviewing *Collected Poems,* said that Sassoon's eye "was in the mind. He had what our forefathers called in-wit; and there can be no continuity in art without it, and little that is worth collecting."14

Sequences

Published in 1956 and dedicated to the novelist-journalist H. M. Tomlinson, *Sequences* is Sassoon's last large collection of new work. Sixty-two short, linguistically spare poems emerged from recent privately published volumes: *Common Chords* (1950), *Emblems of Experience* (1951), and *The Tasking* (1954). In *Sequences* the reader is clearly "in the presence of a religious sensibility of great integrity" (Thorpe, 258). That sensibility had grown closer to the metaphysical seventeenth century than the skeptical twentieth. It is the spirit alone that Sassoon, the developing mystic, now celebrates. Peace has been declared at last.

Sequences's poems are reflections on the state of humanity. The tranquil pieces have "a brooding delicacy that fits particularly close to the thought-rhythms of an ageing, meditative man, his mind and words sharpened by a lifetime of genuine, personal poetry."[15]

"Release," the first poem in *Sequences,* establishes the premise of the collection. Sassoon sets about "to drive . . . up to date" his "much bemused head."[16] His role is prophet, "Forecasting human fate" (*Se,* 3). In "The Unproven" Science listens "outside Eternity for Knowledge / And divination of Death," but "Hushed was Heaven; and all those angels, / Still hopeful, held their breath" (*Se,* 4), waiting for news of life after death.

Sassoon finds "Euphrasy" in the winter of his life. Like Henry Vaughan and George Herbert, Sassoon delights in the perception of infinity that harmonious nature intones. In February the persona knows "the feel of winter finishing once more. . . . Is this then to grow old?" (*Se,* 5). With a few literal images and few words "An Example" provides a moment of insight in which nature teaches tranquillity to the persona. "Dumb patient earth" holds the persona's "unquiet mind from speech" (*Se,* 6) until peace infuses him.

"At Max Gate," Thomas Hardy's home, "provides an amusing sketch of "Old Man Hardy" (*Se,* 7). "The Message" extols, in stunning Wordsworthian language, the extraordinary beauty of a November sunset: "Cloud streaks and shoals, like silver wings outspread / Spanned innocent serenities of blue" (*Se,* 8), and in this way the heavenly "message" is delivered and the "childlike" persona is close to accepting it.

"The Hardened Heart" is the darkest poem in *Sequences,* one of the few that look back to the time when "Youth with morning mind / Went lost (*Se,* 10). Almost as sad, "A Post-Mortem" portrays "post-atomic-warfare man" as a pitiful survivor "Searching for souvenirs among some rubble" (*Se,* 13). As an ironist the persona comments sarcastically, "They got only what they asked for and deserved," but as a Christian he pities "them that only asked for peace" (*Se,* 13).

Even "A 1940 Memory" of "war's worst trouble" (*Se,* 12), however, does not prevent faith in the endurability of life. In "Elsewhere" Sassoon deplores the fact that "nothing one man can think or say" can obviate war, but fortunately "the indestructible exists / Beyond formulas of scientists" (*Se,* 14). And "In Time of Decivilisation" the persona had found spiritual certainty, recognizing, as in Coleridge's "The Eolian Harp," that the poet is "Only as viol to string / Vibrant," and ready to "accord / With time's importuning" (*Se,* 11).

In "Man and Dog" Sassoon honors that ancient symbiosis, while in the ironic "Contemporary Christmas" the "Armageddon of Dark and Light" goes on (*Se*, 16). In "Praise Persistent" and "An Asking" the persona treats humankind's relationship with "the Maker." The persona is "Alone with life" but knows that prayer songs are heard and felt somehow: "Held to what infinite heart—heard by what immanent ear?" (*Se*, 17). He ponders his heritage, while beyond Plato's cave there is "The soul—a star—a gift" (*Se*, 18).

"Resurrection" and "Redemption," metaphysical poems, are homages to Henry Vaughan's "Regeneration." Sassoon's primary concern is the spiritual journey, wherein one day "mystic me" will be able "To stand with those white presences delivered through death" (*Se*, 19), and "Asking no more of Heaven" (*Se*, 20).

"Old-Fashioned Weather," "Early March," "On Scratchbury Camp," and "A Fallodon Memory"—an elegy to the diplomat Sir Edward Grey—are beautiful poems of individual pictoral intelligence, in which the persona finds continuity in nature despite "war's imperious wing" (*Se*, 30). He is "content with the mere fact that fields are drying fast" (*Se*, 29).

"A Proprietor" and "Associates" are self-sketches. Sassoon is the "meditative man. . . . Wondering what manner of men / Will walk [where] Those trees he planted are long fallen or felled" (*Se*, 32). He is now his own friend, "A way-worn man within you dwells / And I am he" (*Se*, 35). A life is a brief episode, and in "Cleaning the Candelabrum" Sassoon lightly meditates on the realization that fine and beautiful furnishings have their own lives and we are only temporary custodians.

"To be sixty is no easy thing," exclaims the persona in "Solitudes at Sixty" (*Se*, 26), while in "Ultimate Values" "The hour grows late, and I outlive my friends" (*Se*, 27). Sassoon is thinking of ghosts again, those long-lost friends. A living friend of 50 years reminds him, "What an old library of life I am!" in "Travelling Library" (*Se*, 24). A rueful, nostalgic humor tones these pieces. Sassoon is reaching, as all must do, toward self-knowledge and a comprehension of mortality. In "Wren and Man" he poignantly states, "Not till that nimble creature knows its name / Will you have learnt your meaning among men" (*Se*, 25).

"Awareness of Alcuin" finds the persona "At peace in my tall-windowed Wiltshire room" (*Se*, 34), translating the verse of Charlemagne's English scholar. Alcuin "sought grace within him" (*Se*, 34), and so does Sassoon. In "Acceptance" the persona has passed through the two early stages of life, "Simpleton, accuser," and has reached "acceptor," where in the presence of the "one deliverer, Death," Man begs, "Take not Thy Holy Spirit from us, Lord" (*Se,* 37). At last Sassoon has left behind the anxieties of his age. His youthful self, the sometimes mawkish sufferer, he hardly recognizes in "A Dream." He says to his shade: "Strange . . . since you and I are one / Let us go back. Let us undo what's done" (*Se,* 36). The need is for grace. The "Befriending Star" must "Empower my human frailty to conceive you kind" (*Se,* 38). That kindness will grant "for my lowly faith, a sign by which to steer" (*Se,* 38). Like Emily Dickinson, Sassoon can no longer keep from dwelling on eternity. In "World without End" the persona has at last come to "trust eternity" (*Se,* 40), and "The Messenger" is God the Friend. The "Mind, busy in the body's life-lit room" (*Se,* 41), must listen to the soul, with which God communicates. "The Present Writer," reclusive in his "thought-haunted room," now waits without remorse for looming "Departure and disfleshment" (*Se,* 42).

"The Tasking," "The Question," and the sonnet "The Making" deal with the persona's need to "put world sounds behind and hope to hear / Instructed spirit speaking" (*Se,* 45). He is "Eternity's quick creature" (*Se,* 48), realizing that "This making is a mystery" (*Se,* 49). In "Faith Unfaithful" the persona moves "Toward ungranted God" (*Se,* 51). "Retreat from Eternity" and "The Dispersal" ask the "Universal," "How do you handle my dispersal?" (*Se,* 50), and whether "stellar space" and "one human face" (*Se,* 46) are bridgeable concepts. "The Visitant," in its search for an understanding of the nature of self, reads like pieces by Gerard Manley Hopkins in such lines as "Clocked occluded self wrote never lines like his" (*Se,* 47).

"Another Spring," "The Half Century," and "The Welcoming" are poems of youth and aging. "Aged self, disposed to lose his hold on life, / Looks down, at winter's ending, and perceives / Continuance in some crinkled primrose leaves" (*Se,* 56), yet "Age, reading in the book of life," does so with "ruth" (*Se,* 57). Still, youth is marveled at, "Umblemished and unbelieving" (*Se,* 58). Mature man, in "The Worst of It," empowered by armaments of flame" (*Se,* 59), is fallen. The persona is removed from Promethean folly: "Here's Me; who neither ask nor aim to be / More than the mote in heaven's revealéd ray" (*Se,* 59). But in "The Best of It" the persona asserts that "Life . . . by no disaster is undone" and that there is "Star-sown eternity for mindsight old" (*Se,* 60). In "The Humble Heart" the persona sends his soul "seeking" to "Blood and bone befriend . . . till withdrawn to share some timeless quest" (*Se,* 67), for although as in "Human Bondage" the persona remains "Prisoned and impassioned by my clay" (*Se,* 62), he knows "a universe beyond me" (*Se,* 62).

"An Epitome" shouts, *"Accept your soul"* (*Se,* 63), and "Renewals" advises, "Put discontents behind; / Be silent and grow still" (*Se,* 64). The old persona merges with "October Trees," joining "Your foliaged farewell" (*Se,* 65). In "Sic Sedebat" ("Thus He Sat") the mind and the body retreat: "Little enough you've learnt / While being within you burnt" (*Se,* 66). Now "Little the mind remembers" (*Se,* 66). The final poem in *Sequences,* "A Chord," again affirms the transcendental nature of art with grace: "on stillness came a chord, / While I, the instrument, knew long-withheld reward" (*Se,* 68).

After *Counter-Attack* and *Picture-Show, Sequences* is Sassoon's finest individual collection of poetry. Distilled and bereft of appetite, with the ocherous tint of early Georgianism washed out, the poems show the poet-persona squarely facing the eternal tomorrow, while "the long-felt desire for spiritual certainty has been answered" (Thorpe, 245).

The Path to Peace

In 1960 Sassoon privately published *The Path to Peace,* a collection of 29 poems dedicated to Mary Immaculate, all but 6 of which had been previously published in collections public and private, including the recent *Lenten Illuminations* (1958). The selection and raison d'être is to present a retrospective documenting the poet's spiritual journey, from pantheism, through doubt, to full faith, over a lifetime of poetry from 1909 to 1960. This path for Sassoon was the road to Roman Catholicism.

The new poems, written between 1957 and 1960, are, like the rest, devotional pieces. "Rogation" is Latinate, labored, and alliterative, as the persona seeks "Concord no sanctity could comprehend, / Mercy immeasurable and multiplied."[17] In "Deliverance" the persona finds comfort after looking "Beyond the darkened thickets of my brain" (*PP,* 25). The persona laments, in "Arbor Vitae," that "This tree all winter through / Found no green work to do" (*PP,* 27). The poem is as simple and as moving as a medieval ballad. "Unfoldment" delicately draws a homile from daffodil buds unsheathing themselves in a warm room, where "The lamp's their sun" (*PP,* 28). "A Prayer at Pentecost" is to the "Master musician, Life," asking it to "Be noteless now. Our dualogue is done" (*PP,* 31).

Written last, in November 1960, "Awaitment" has the persona asking to "be lost; and lose myself in Thee" (*PP,* 30–31). Sassoon is very near his goal: "Let me be found; and find my soul set free" (*PP,* 30–31).

An Octave

In celebration of Sassoon's eightieth birthday and financed by subscription, *An Octave* was published on 8 September 1966. The collection is a tribute from friends and admirers, including W. H. Auden, John Betjeman, Edmund Blunden, C. Day Lewis, Roy Fuller, Robert Graves, Philip Larkin, John Lehmann, John Masefield, Herbert Read, Jon Silkin, and Stephen Spender. The eight poems were written during the seven years following 1957, the year Sassoon was received into the Roman Catholic church, and are testaments of faith.

Two poems in *An Octave* were new to the collection. "Proven Purpose" has the persona denying any existence "but in thy Being."[18] "A Prayer in Old Age" is a moving farewell to life and a humble greeting to the life to come: "My nothingness must kneel below Thy Cross. / There let new life begin" (*O, 8*). Sassoon ended his career and his life in full submission and devotion.

Sassoon's later poetry is generally quiet, lamely satiric, and succeedingly devotional. It celebrates nature, the past, memory, and the human spirit. The religious poetry is gentle and modest. Poetics are traditional, forms are simple, and diction is direct. Without intellectual tours de force, linguistic pyrotechnics, or coloratura runs of iterative imagery, Sassoon's later poetry is minor, but it is neither faint nor false. In the end, talking to God turned out to be the best way for him to talk to us.

Chapter Five

George Sherston

"Suddenly, towards the end of the 20's, the blocked-up dam of bad memories, nightmares, trauma had burst and memoirs, volumes of letters, novels, autobiographies and other troops . . . centred books started to pour torrentially forth," notes Valentine Cunningham.[1] It had taken 10 years for the simmering pot of black memory to boil over and for a war-sick European and American public to become interested in the conflict once more. The first flood included Siegfried Sassoon's *Memoirs of a Fox-hunting Man* (1928), Edmund Blunden's *Undertones of War* (1928), R. C. Sheriff's drama *Journey's End* (1928), Robert Graves's *Good-bye to All That* (1929), Richard Aldington's *Death of a Hero* (1929), Ernest Hemingway's *A Farewell to Arms* (1929), and Erich Maria Remarque's *All Quiet on the Western Front* (1928; English translation 1929).

World War I had left Sassoon wounded in body and mind, nervous, exhausted, grieving, sleepless, and unhappy. His self-prescribed remedy was simple. He embarked "on the obsessive enterprise which occupied most of the rest of his life, the revisiting of the war and the contrasting world before the war in a series of six volumes of artful memoirs" (Fussell, 91). The first three volumes are fictionalized autobiography: *Memoirs of a Fox-hunting Man* (1928), *Memoirs of an Infantry Officer* (1930), and *Sherston's Progress* (1936), subsequently published in a one-volume edition as *The Complete Memoirs of George Sherston* (1937). Three volumes of pure autobiography followed, the subjects of the next chapter.

In *The Complete Memoirs of George Sherston* Sassoon evokes a memory of late Victorian and Edwardian upper-class life from about 1895 to 1918, and the impact of the war on a representative of that class. Other post–World War I writers also chose to remain, imaginatively, in the late Victorian–Edwardian era in order to avoid fully facing the disorienting postwar world. Ivy Compton-Burnett is a case in point. It is understandable that sensitive souls, having seen the beastliness of life, can recoil from it by re-creating the world of their childhood and youth. Sassoon, an old soldier, took cover in the past. He needed his own *À la recherche du temps perdu*. To write is both to remember and to forget. It is exercise and exorcism.

82

Memoirs of a Fox-hunting Man

Memoirs of a Fox-hunting Man was published anonymously, but the public quickly realized Sassoon was the author of the first-person autobiographical novel. There have been confusion and controversy over the nature of the trilogy. It is not autobiography, even though the characters and incidents are taken from experience, with names and places only marginally changed, and it can be viewed as a roman à clef, but tone, texture, structure, plot, and central characterization are fictive. Readers interested in the real-life models or counterparts of various characters in *The Complete Memoirs of George Sherston* may consult Rupert Hart-Davis's edition of *Siegfried Sassoon's Diaries 1915–1918* (1983).

Memoirs of a Fox-hunting Man is a celebration of the pleasures of youth, set in and about that loveliest of pastoral settings, the English country estate, frequently explored in literature, as in the elegant *The Country House* (1907) of John Galsworthy. It is also a celebration of sports: cricket, horse-racing, and particularly fox-hunting, in the tradition of the nineteenth-century novelist Robert Smith Surtees.[2]

Four-fifths of *Memoirs of a Fox-hunting Man* is a pastoral remembrance, a romance salted with ironic and satiric touches as Sassoon looks back to a more innocent time through the eyes of George Sherston, innocent himself, snobbish, hero-worshiping, and moved only by horses and hunting. He, unlike his creator, is neither poet nor musician. The text exudes a sense of longing for the days of trifles instead of rifles. The last fifth of the book begins in August 1914, with Sherston in the army going to France and losing his best friend, "Dick Tiltwood," in life, David Thomas.

George's progress begins in childhood at his Aunt Evelyn's country house. He is an orphan without a role-model male relative, no brother or uncle. He is initiated into the "sport" of fox-hunting by the insistent, avuncular groom Dixon. Eventually George becomes an excellent horseman, even winning the climactic point-to-point race, the Colonel's Cup. He also makes friends and wins the respect of the Master of the Hounds, whom he idolizes.

The bildungsroman documents "the stages of a young man's initiation into the tribal rites of the English country gentry" (Knox, 144). George lives in bucolic Kent on an allowance of £600 per year. Fox-hunting is hard for him at first because he is a sensitive youth, and he must brutalize his feelings toward the quarry, although he makes no kill and goes to war innocent of any blood. The red-coated fraternity, however, is extremely conservative, politically and socially, and George must also adapt to their selfishness, self-absorption, chauvinism, and disdain for the lower classes. Typically his education is desultory, and although he goes up to Cambridge he quits without a degree.

George's greatest affection is for his horse, Cockbird; there are no girls in his life. After winning the Colonel's Cup he becomes something of a celebrity in his limited circle, and friendships blossom with young men of his class, such as Stephen Colwood, whom he first met at school. When 1914 arrives, Stephen is in the artillery, and George, feeling incompetent, turns down opportunities to be commissioned, enlisting instead as a private in the cavalry, the natural extension of his horsey life. Thrown from a mount and having broken his arm, and tired of "raking up horse-dung before breakfast," George asks to be commissioned in the infantry. The day of the horse is over for him and, symbolically, for the world. At the army camp he meets Dick Tiltwood, and the friendship grows fast and deep. George learns that Stephen has been killed in action, and the subsequent death of Dick leaves him distraught. At his own request George is sent to the trenches, where, like a caveman with a club, he waits, as the novel ends, to kill Germans: "And here I was, with my knobkerrie in my hand, staring across at the enemy I'd never seen. Somewhere out of sight beyond the splintered tree-tops of Hidden Wood a bird had begun to sing. Without knowing why, I remembered that it was Easter Sunday. Standing in that dismal ditch, I could find no consolation in the thought that Christ was risen. I sploshed back to the dug-out to call the others up for 'stand-to.'"[3] In war nature's grace is a mockery and Christ's sacrifice is for naught.

George learns about life from those varied experiences which come his way, as all youth must. He comes to know his own strengths and limitations, while success in sports gives him confidence and helps bring him to maturity. He grows to understand human frailty and the truth of mortality. He learns self-criticism, and he learns that his fellow hunters are often poor riders, that those who talk much often do little, and that vanity, incompetence, and stupidity are everywhere. Sassoon offers frequent satiric observations, such as the description of Lieutenant Colonel C. M. F. Hesmon, Retired, "a widower for many years," who is all bridles, bits, and boots. In his stables

elegant green stable-buckets (with the Colonel's numerous initials painted on them in white) were arranged at regular intervals along the walls, and the harness-room was hung with enough bits and bridles to stock a saddler's shop. It was . . . a regular museum of mouth gear. For the Colonel was one of those fussy riders with indifferent hands who are always trying their horses with a new bit. "I haven't found the key to this mare's mouth yet," he would say, as the irritated animal shook its head and showered everyone within range with flecks of froth. And when he got home from hunting he would say to his confidential old head-groom: "I think this mare's still a bit under-bitted, Dumbrell," and they would debate over half the bits in the harness-room before he rode the mare again. . . . Along the wall stood an astonishing array of hunting-boots. These struck me as being so numerous that I had the presence of mind to count them. There were twenty-seven pairs. Now a good pair of top-boots, if properly looked after and repaired, will last the owner a good many years; and a new pair once in three years might be considered a liberal allowance for a man who has started with two or three pairs. But the Colonel was nothing if not regular in his habits; every autumn he visited, with the utmost solemnity, an illustrious boot-maker in Oxford Street; and each impeccable little pair of boots had signalized the advent of yet another opening meeting. And, since the Colonel seldom hunted more than three days a week, they had consequently accumulated." (*FHM,* 163–65)

George's perceptive eye also notes that the Colonel "had the appearance of a man who had been left behind. . . . Elderly people looked like that during the War, when they had said good-bye to someone and the train had left them alone on the station platform" (*FHM,* 126–127). Sassoon frequently reminds readers that they are looking back across the chasm of World War I. Sherston comes to understand "the antithesis of peace and war" in *Memoirs of a Fox-hunting Man* (Onions, 136). In translating Sherston from happy hunter to unhappy warrior Sassoon has raised his narrative from romance to allegory. The novel is replete with satire, irony, nostalgia, and myth. Robert Graves sums up his old comrade's story curiously but appropriately: "He leaves his readers to decide for him whether the book is sincere or ironical. So it had often been with him, I think."[4]

Memoirs of a Fox-hunting Man contains Sassoon's best prose. It won the Hawthornden Prize, and it established his reputation as a fine crafter of prose, thus providing Sassoon with a 20-year audience for his semiauto-biographical and, later, purely autobiographical writing.

Memoirs of an Infantry Officer

Perhaps only Sassoon, recollecting in tranquillity, could have turned the experience of bitterest battle into a picture of color and music—not a pretty picture, but art nevertheless. In *Memoirs of an Infantry Officer* war is seen through a countryman's eyes and a poet's imagination. The novel's main theme is the inevitability of war and the concomitant futility of resisting it, for that ancient plague of humankind is to Sassoon a continuing "breach of order and harmony upon earth" (Thorpe, 92).

Sherston matures further in *Memoirs of an Infantry Officer.* He is prepared to die, even expectant, and soldiering makes him democratic. He learns that suffering is ever the soldier's portion. He sees the heroism of the common soldiers, who are brave not because they are under orders but because of their indomitable human courage, created by the very horror they were required to endure. Sherston says, "I was rewarded by an intense memory of men whose courage had shown me the power of the human spirit—that spirit which could withstand the utmost assault. . . . Against the background of the War and its brutal stupidity those men had stood glorified by the thing which sought to destroy them."[5]

Memoirs of an Infantry Officer opens quietly, allowing more power and effectiveness for the crescendo of battle to come. It is spring 1916 and Sherston, in the trenches, has made up his mind to die. Seeing him depressed, his colonel sends him to the Fourth Army Camp at Flixécourt for a month's training in open warfare, under the assumption that a breakthrough is imminent. The instructors have had no combat experience themselves, and so have little credibility.

Returning to his battalion, Sherston is involved in a disastrous raid on the opposing trenches. He goes into no-man's-land to help bring out the casualties. Later the newspaper account of the debacle falsely reports the raid as a success.

Sherston is given leave and finds life in Britain a strange and uncomfortable contrast to "England in France." A big push, the Battle of the Somme, is in the offering, and, surprisingly, everyone at home knows the "secret." When Sherston informs Aunt Evelyn that he is anticipating receiving the Military Cross, she is shocked because she believed her nephew was in the transport service.

Returning to France via London, Lieutenant Sherston buys combat gear because the government-issue equipment is so poor. When the Somme offensive begins, his company moves forward in confusion and gets lost behind the lines. His company finally in position, Sherston is maddened by the shooting of a friend and goes over the top with Mills bombs, capturing a German trench single-handedly, but then does not know what to do with it. On his return to British lines his colonel remonstrates, "Why hadn't I consolidated Wood Trench? Why the hell hadn't I sent back a message to let him know that it had been occupied? I made no attempt to answer these conundrums. Obviously I'd made a mess of the whole affair" (*IO*, 93).

Sherston then meets his army friend and fellow officer David Cromlech, modeled after Robert Graves, and they share experiences. Shortly after the Battle of the Somme commences Sherston comes down with enteritis and is evacuated to a hospital in Oxford. There he recovers and is able to spend time at home with his aunt and the local fox hunts, but then he must return to France. In the Battle of Arras he receives a neck wound. In England again and under the influence of politically and socially important pacifists, he rebels against the direction of the war by the establishment. Guided by Thornton Tyrrell, a pacifist philosopher, modeled after Bertrand Russell, Sherston protests the war in writing, expecting court-martial and possibly execution, but his superiors choose not to regard him seriously. He goes before a medical board and, thanks to David Cromlech's conniving and convincing, is sent to "Slateford War Hospital," diagnosed as shell-shocked. Before leaving he "ripped the Military Cross ribbon off my tunic and threw it into the mouth of the Mersey" (*IO*, 315).

Memoirs of an Infantry Officer attempts to make art as well as order out of chaos. In that sense it is like all war novels, trying to replace horror, hatred, savagery, and indignation with irony, satire, compassion, and understanding:

I noticed an English soldier lying by the road with a horribly smashed head; soon such sights would be too frequent to attract attention, but this first one was perceptibly unpleasant. At the risk of being thought squeamish or even unsoldierly, I still maintain that an ordinary human being has a right to be momentarily horrified by a mangled body seen on an afternoon walk, although people with sound common sense can always refute me by saying that life is full of gruesome sights and violent catastrophes. But I am no believer in wild denunciations of the War; I am merely describing my own experiences of it; and in 1917 I was only beginning to learn that life, for the majority of the population, is an unlovely struggle against unfair odds, culminating in a cheap funeral. (*IO*, 201)

Sassoon has Sherston sounding like Hobbes.

Sassoon finds many satiric opportunities in *Memoirs of an Infantry Officer*. Staff officers and rear-echelon personnel, as well as civilians, feel the sting of his lash. The bloodthirsty Scottish major of the Fourth Army school is savagely sketched: "The star turn . . . was a massive sandy-haired Highland Major whose subject was 'The Spirit of the Bayonet.' Though at that time undecorated, he was afterwards awarded the D.S.O. for lecturing. He took as his text a few leading points from the *Manual of Bayonet Training.* . . . He spoke with homicidal eloquence. . . . Man, it seemed, had been created to jab the life out of Germans. To hear the Major talk, one might have thought that he did it himself every day before breakfast" (*IO,* 14–15).

Memoirs of an Infantry Officer does not universalize war. For the soldiers and sailors involved it is always an individual experience. Sassoon merely wanted to show the effect of the war on an ordinary human being with whom the reader could identify. Sassoon's "hero," Sherston, is a basic Englishman, representative of his class, who reacts, with a kind of expected, regular courage, to events he has no control over, both in the war against the Germans and the war against the war.

Correspondingly the war has little effect on nature, which remains, as in Auden's "Musée des Beaux Arts," sublimely indifferent to human ambition, stupidity, and folly. After attending the vile lecture on bayoneting Germans, Sherston "went up the hill to my favorite sanctuary, a wood of hazels and beeches. The evening air smelt of wet mold and wet leaves; the trees were misty-green. . . . Peace was there in the twilight of that prophetic foreign spring" (*IO,* 16). A great charm of George Sherston is that he is the consummate "Georgian."

War and antiwar are antithetically opposed in *Memoirs of an Infantry Officer,* and they neutralize each other. Sherston proceeds from the prison of the military to the prison of the medical. Sassoon is highly critical of his protagonist's inability to affect war or effect peace.

Sherston's Progress

Artistically *Sherston's Progress* is the least satisfactory section of the trilogy. The novel seems rushed, and the novelist tired of the work, but realizing that he must finish what he started some seven years before. For the first time in the trilogy Sassoon began to think of his experiences in archetypal terms. He made the connection between his western front and Eliot's *The Waste Land* (1922), and by titling the third novel *Sherston's Progress* he reminds his readers that Sherston's journey into and out of no-man's-land is like the journey of Christian in Bunyan's *The Pilgrim's Progress,* from the City of Destruction to the City of Zion, a story nearly all knew from childhood. George Sherston is a simple seeker like Christian, and at the end he, like Christian, understands what his goal has been—to comprehend self: "My last words shall be these—that it is only from the inmost silences of the heart that we know the world for what it is, and ourselves for what the world has made us."[6]

In *Sherston's Progress* George no longer hopes for the reformation of the collective conscience regarding the war. It seems it must be accepted as the permanent natural state of existence: confined living in a mortuary. When promoted to captain, Sherston tries to be the best company officer he can be and to do everything to save the lives of his charges: "but all I can do for them is to try and obtain them fresh vegetables with my own money, and teach them how to consolidate shell holes" (*SPr*, 177). He has learned that "One cannot be a useful officer and a reader of imaginative literature at the same time. Efficiency depends on attention to a multitude of minor details" (*SPr*, 195).

Sherston's Progress begins in the summer of 1917 at "Slateford War Hospital" for shell-shocked victims, where Sherston, to his surprise, meets a compassionate military doctor, Captain W. H. R. Rivers (one of the very few actual names in the trilogy), a neurologist with great human sympathy, understanding, and professional ability. They become good friends. Kind treatment, good food, and golf ease Sherston's apprehensions and anxieties. In autumn he begins to feel ashamed that his convictions, genuine though they are, have given him shelter from the whirlwind in France. He sees the ghosts of dead comrades, and he "visualized an endless column of marching soldiers, singing 'Tipperary' on their way up from the back areas; I saw them filing silently along ruined roads, and lugging their bad boots through mud until they came to some shell hole and pillar-box line in a landscape where trees were stumps and skeletons and no Quartermaster on earth could be certain of getting the rations up. . . . The idea of going back there was indeed like death" (*SPr*, 43). Nevertheless guilt and a sense of destiny win out. Ironically, he convinces himself "that going back to the War as soon as possible was my only chance of peace" (*SPr*, 44).

In November a medical board restores him to active duty. After service in Ireland, Egypt, and Palestine he is posted to the western front once more, as the German successes of March 1918 have led to a crisis for the Allies. In May he is back at the Fourth Army school, listening "to the famous lecture on 'The Spirit of the Bayonet.' The brawny Scotchman, now a Colonel, addressed two battalions from a farm wagon in a bright-green field. His lecture is the same as it was two years ago" (*SPr*,

169). Nothing has changed in the year he was out of France, except that hundreds of thousands more have been killed.

Captain Sherston at age 31 is an "old soldier" now, a remarkable survivor. In the trenches again, he takes more and more risks, seeming to court death. Finally, he goes out on an unnecessary night patrol, and on his return to the British line is accidentally shot in the head by one of his own sergeants, mistaking him for an enemy. The absurdities and waste of war!

Sherston thinks he has been fatally wounded and is almost happy and content with the gesture of sacrifice. But the wound is not mortal, and once more he is evacuated to England. Despondent over the anticlimactic end to his search for martyrdom, he is restored to mental health by Dr. Rivers. "Oh Rivers," he says, on first viewing the good doctor entering his room, "I've had such a funny time since I saw you last!" (*SPr,* 245). Funny "odd" and funny "hysterical." And *The Complete Memoirs of George Sherston* concludes not with a melodramatic bang but with a boy's whimpering astonishment.

Sherston's Progress is weakened in the middle because of an unusual auctorial intrustion. Sassoon inserts 73 diarylike pages into the narrative, so that the reader feels fiction has been interrupted and temporarily replaced by notes and outline. Another oddity is that Sherston and his fellow soldiers do little or no killing: their business, after all. They are mostly passive recipients of shot and shell, waiting stoically, perhaps even masochistically. Their relative inaction can be partly explained by physical exhaustion, depression, and being "ping-ponged" between the unrelenting, ironic polarities of war: friend and foe, night work and day rest, friendly trenches and enemy trenches, visible comrades and invisible enemies, France and England, unbearable noise and eerie silence, terror and boredom, young life and sudden death, and so on.

The Complete Memoirs of George Sherston is an everyman's journey from the hopes and shallow triumphs of youth, through the valley of the shadow of death, to the realization that the world is a hospital and a charnel. Sherston's terrible experiences test and develop his character. These experiences are extrapolated into an examined life.

Sassoon's *The Complete Memoirs of George Sherston* and Richard Aldington's *Death of a Hero* are the two great British World War I combat novels. Aldington's hero, Winterbourne, is a mature, happily married man at the beginning of the war. His journey is an existential fall to disorientation and meaningless death. Sherston matures from youth to manhood, his character is fired in the kiln of war, and a capacity to endure emerges. *Death of a Hero* is an existential tragedy. *The Complete Memoirs of George Sherston* ends with a ray of hope for the survivors of the generational slaughter. In neither novel is the horror of battle ever treated as a cliché. Sassoon's great achievement, however, is the creation of a fictional character who became more real than life, as he symbolized his generation, his class, and his painful time.

Chapter Six

Siegfried Redux

The Autobiographies

One year after the publication of *The Complete Memoirs of George Sherston* Sassoon began to relive and rewrite his life once more, this time in three straight autobiographies, starting with infancy: *The Old Century and Seven More Years* (1938), covering his childhood, school, and university years, 1886–1907; *The Weald of Youth* (1942), dealing with his country life and early London literary life, 1909–14; and *Siegfried's Journey, 1916–1920* (1945), the story of his wartime and immediate postwar literary experiences, 1914–20.

It is significant that Sassoon began his autobiographical trilogy as Europe went to war again, first in Spain in 1936 and then throughout the Continent and the world in 1939. Indeed in *Siegfried's Journey 1916–1920* he wrote about one war in the midst of another. Autobiography provided Sassoon with relief from the terrible present. Clearly he had decided that the years of his life worth remembering were those of his youth and early manhood, war and all, 1886–1920. Including *The Complete Memoirs of George Sherston* and the three autobiographies, Sassoon spent almost 20 years writing about his earlier life.

The great significance of Sassoon's autobiographies, as Arthur E. Lane points out, is that, along with Graves's and Blunden's memoirs, "they are our best prose record of a poet's personal involvement in the Great War" (Lane, 92–93). Beyond the scope of Graves and Blunden, they also project and codify, with nostalgia, a genteel, slow-paced, orderly, country, upper-class way of life in an old England long changed, but, thanks to Sassoon, not forgotten.

The Old Century and Seven More Years

Of the three autobiographies *The Old Century and Seven More Years* is generally considered the superior. Its gift is "the love of nature and country life" (Thorpe, 256). Sassoon's prophet was Thomas Hardy. In an

92

oblique way, with its love and fascination for the late nineteenth-century English manor house and country estate, *The Old Century and Seven More Years* is an homage to the master of the English rural novel. But contrary to Hardy's, Sassoon's view is totally positive. The book breathes a deep longing for the late Victorian and Edwardian past, a time of seemingly perpetual summer, when a privileged young man could believe that he was the center of the universe, with mother, aunts, uncles, friends, servants, and all the world revolving around him in concentric circles.

Sassoon's mastery of prose, first indicated in *Memoirs of a Fox-hunting Man,* continues and grows in *The Old Country and Seven More Years.* Lines are rhythmic, cadences are finely measured, passion is under control, and the imagery is often exquisite, as in this passage describing a memory of nine years of age:

The year '95 began with freezing cold weather which lasted for nearly two months. There was any amount of snow, and great was our excitement when the red-painted sledge was brought out of the stable barn, and my mother drove her two ponies tandem along the glossy rutted lanes with all three of us snuggling in beside her, and the big sheepskin rug drawn up to our chins and our woolly tam-o'-shanters pulled down to our noses. The bells jingled merrily as we went gliding crisply on until we arrived at the Furnace Pond, which was half a mile long and no one knew for certain how deep. Admiringly we watched Mamsy put on her skates and strike confidently out across the black well-swept ice to join a group of local gentry who were either practising the outside edge or totteringly attempting to achieve it. She looked as free as a bird, skating away from all her worries to cut figures of eight. (*Oc,* 32)

Moved by Sassoon's descriptive prose, David Garnett says of *The Old Century and Seven More Years,* "One can hear the pony trotting down the road, the butcher boy hitting a six on the village green—in a world that knew no fear or doubts and was as blandly delighted with Uncle John's torpedo-boat and destroyers as it was with Uncle Hamo's statues."[1]

Sassoon is remarkably able to capture the language patterns and imaginative expression of the child, the adolescent, and the young adult. From the beginning young Siegfried shows a great sensitivity to human loss through separation, as per his father, and death—his father and Grandmother Thornycroft. He has pity for his invalid, dying Uncle Beer and for Beer's wife, Aunt Rachel. A sensitive and decent human being is in the making: "My intention in this book has been to commemorate or memorialize those human contacts which supported me in my rather simple-minded belief that the world was full of extremely nice people if only one could get to know them properly" (*OC,* 228).

The Old Century and Seven More Years begins with Sassoon's earliest memory of his childhood in Kent, that rural district with enchanting qualities. Sassoon introduces his mother and two brothers, and the reader learns that his father is not present after 1891. Theresa Thornycroft Sassoon is lovingly portrayed as a doting mother, a painter, an athletic person, and a horsewoman of considerable skill. She is unhappy because of her husband's desertion, but she carries on to the best of her ability, providing as normal a life for her sons as she can. *The Old Century and Seven More Years* clearly indicates that Sassoon's childhood was basically happy. Theresa received help and moral support from her brother Hamo, the noted sculptor, who befriended young Siegfried.

"Mamsy" organized poetry readings for her sons, and at 14 Siegfried "vaguely believed that I was going to be a poet" (*OC,* 68). Theresa had confidence in Siegfried's ability as a poet from the beginning and fully encouraged him. She did not approve of schools, and so Siegfried was tutored at home until he was sent to Marlborough and then Cambridge. Even as a schoolboy and a college student he was frequently at home and happiest there. His mother and the beautiful, mysterious, ancient Weald of Kent, a garden of sensibility, remained a source of inspiration for the youthful versifier. The autobiography shows the power of the landscape on both the young, aspiring poet and the mature writer of the narrative, always avoiding, however, any observation or statement the youth would be incapable of making at the age depicted.

Siegfried's reading carried his imagination to distant realms. H. Rider Haggard took him to the banks of the Zambesi, and H. G. Wells made him a time traveler. Relatives, family friends, and servants produced deep impressions on Siegfried, and Sassoon describes them with affection and great skill. Most interesting and important is "Wirgie," his mother's friend, who tutored Siegfried, taught him piano, and encouraged his writing, and with whom the young Siegfried identified, although she was 40 years his elder. Others finely described are Uncle John Thornycroft, a famous naval engineer; Mr. Moon, the tutor, affectionately called "Moony"; Ellen Batty, another friend of his mother and a long-serving, affectionate tutor; and several others.

Cambridge proved to be a disaster for Siegfried and a tragedy for his family. At college he suffered from lack of interest, lack of motivation, aimlessness, indecision, and conflicting advice. He had been sent to cramming school. Special tutors had been hired. The family had connections. But Siegfried had no academic desire. Expected by his family to read for the bar after graduation, he tried studying law but hated it. He switched to history, but it was just as boring. Then he tried unsuccessfully to win the Chancellor's Medal in poetry. What Siegfried really wanted to do at college, besides writing verse and playing sports, was to collect books: "What I aimed at was a large cozy accumulation of leather-bound tomes" (*OC,* 204).

Siegfried leaves Cambridge, sans degree, with feelings of freedom and relief. He is happy. He has a purpose in life: to be a poet. *The Old Century and Seven More Years* ends on Sassoon's twenty-first birthday: "This September morning looked as if nothing could change its meridian prosperity. As I turned to go up to the house, I couldn't imagine what it would feel like to be more than twenty-one. Lucky to be in love with life, I did not know how lucky I was" (*OC,* 267).

The Old Century and Seven More Years is a highly finished painting of idyllic country life, depicted in soft, rosy tones. It is full of happy memories. The fragrances of May pervade it. The sounds of quarreling sparrows, the gentle rain on windowpanes, the hum of insects in foliage, and the soft whistle of a rural train provide syncopation. Dark clouds are far beyond the horizon in this rich portrait of the artist as a young man.

The Weald of Youth

The Weald of Youth deals with Sassoon's twenty-third to twenty-eighth years, and its main theme is the growth of a poet, one whose life, in that it was so privileged and fortunate, seems unsuited for the development of a sensitive writer. Wisely Sassoon treats these formative years lightly.

The young man portrayed in *The Weald of Youth* has a split personality. As a countryman he is confident and courageous, riding to the hounds, racing furiously, competing successfully in cricket and golf. As a neophyte poet he is tentative and diffident. He has his poems printed privately and expensively, sometimes destroying the publications when despondent over his ability and limited progress as a poet. The poet seems to get in the way of the sportsman, causing unrest if not unhappiness. Simultaneously, writing satisfies a need the outdoor life is unable to do: "Poetry was a dream world into which I escaped through an esoteric door in my mind" (*WY,* 28).

The *Weald of Youth* begins with the 23-year-old trying to break into the literary world, although still living at home in Weirleigh. After several rejections by editors, some of his sonnets are accepted for publication by a minor periodical called the *Academy*, whose editor, the shadowy T. W. H. Crosland, summons Sassoon to London for a meeting, thus opening up, ever so slightly, a new world for Sassoon. Crosland promises Sassoon high prices for his poems but in fact does pay him, for Crosland is a vanity publisher, looking to profit from poets trying to have their books published. Sassoon had already gone that route twice before, with little recognition forthcoming. Uncle Hamo, however, encouraged Sassoon to send one of his collections to a distinguished family friend, the literary lion Edmund Gosse, who "responded with a letter of lively encouragement" (*WY* 17), fulsomely praising the poetic masque *Orpheus in Diloeryum*, which reminded him "of the strange entertainments of the early Renaissance, and of Italian humanism generally" (*WY*, 17). The poorly educated Sassoon wonders, "What exactly *was* Italian humanism?" (*WY*, 17). The young poet's response, of course, was to send more poems.

Invited to his first Gosse "At Home," Sassoon is most concerned with his apparel: "My appearance, I felt, was creditable enough, for I was wearing my buff linen waistcoat, with spats to match, and there was nothing countrified about my irreproachable dark summer suit" (*WY*, 89–90). In fact, despite his tony outfit and his gentry background, he is a country bumpkin.

Connections, however, meant a great deal in Edwardian London. Gosse's encouragement leads to Sassoon's writing the parody of Masefield, *The Daffodil Murderer*, which Gosse sends to Edward Marsh, the editor of *Georgian Poetry* and, in Gosse's words, "the choragus of the new poets" (*WY*, 126). Marsh invites Sassoon to visit, and they become mentor and disciple. During an evening tête-à-tête in Marsh's flat in Gray's Inn, the older man advises Sassoon to take rooms in London, and "When he suggested Gray's Inn I knew the matter was as good as settled, and left my scruples to take care of themselves" (*WY*, 182). The young sportsman is out of place, however, and very lonely in London. He has little to do beyond writing poetry. Like a tourist, he visits museums, galleries, and the zoo, and calls on writers at home.

Happily Sassoon bumps into Rupert Brooke, who is on his way to Marsh's flat, where he is temporarily abiding. He joyously remarks: "So I've really seen the wonderful Rupert at last" (*WY*, 206). But Sassoon is sad when he compares his lack of success with his exact contemporary's meteoric career. Marsh, though, brings them together a couple of days later at breakfast, and Sassoon "got the impression that the great Rupert Brooke was quite a modest chap after all. . . . He was wearing an open-necked blue shirt and old grey flannel trousers, with sandals on bare feet, and hadn't bothered to brush his brown-gold hair, which was, I thought, just a shade longer than it need have been. Seen in the full light as he sat beside the window, his eyes were a living blue and his face was still sunburnt from outdoor life on a Pacific Island" (*WY,* 209).

Sassoon is envious and admiring, but Brooke pays little attention to him. After Marsh and the other guest, the poet W. H. Davies, leave, Brooke and Sassoon are alone for a half-hour, but Brooke "sat by a window serenely observing the trees of Gray's Inn gardens. From time to time his eyes met mine, but it was with a clouded though direct regard. . . . I am afraid he was also a little bored with me" (*WY,* 114). Soon Sassoon realized that "I was only one more in the procession of people who were more interested in him than he was in them" (*WY,* 215). The impressionable Sassoon is awed and perhaps infatuated: "[It] was my assured perception that I was in the presence of one on whom had been conferred all the invisible attributes of a poet. To this his radiant good looks seemed subsidiary" (*WY,* 216). Sassoon recognizes that Brooke's "intellectual development was years ahead of me, and his character was much more fully formed than mine. I was still slowly unlearning the immaturities which he had got rid of before he was twenty-one. From me as I then was, he could have acquired nothing" (*WY,* 216).

In truth the meeting with Brooke was important to Sassoon's motivation as a poet. The rival poet's presence and attitude were a challenge and a silent reproach: "When bidding me good-bye at Eddie's outer door his demeanour implied that as far as he was concerned there was no apparent reason why we should ever meet again. He may have breathed a sigh of relief at having got rid of me at last" (*WY,* 217). They never met again.

Writing out the formative event almost 30 years later, Sassoon notes both the value of the meeting and a certain ironic aspect that colors it: "There is no need to explain that our one brief meeting had a quite unpredictable significance. Nor need I underline the latent irony of the situation" (*WY,* 217). The irony, of course, is that Brooke would soon be dead, his life, career, and critical reputation cut down by war, while Sassoon would survive and develop into a major writer of his generation.

Tired of cultural days and literary evenings, and with war looming, Sassoon, as much out of boredom as purpose, mounts his bike and cycles 30 miles to Rye to join the cavalry: "The years of my youth were going down for ever in the weltering western gold, and the future would take me far from that sunset-embered horizon. Beyond the night was my new beginning. The Weald had been the world of my youngness, and while I gazed across it now I felt prepared to do what I could to defend it. And after all, dying for one's native land was to be the most glorious thing one could possibly do!" (*WY*, 259).

One of the major attractions of this "gentle revisitation" of days that are no more is Sassoon's deft character sketches, like that of Rupert Brooke. Most fascinating is the shady editor Crosland, whom the naive Siegfried is trying to fathom. Sassoon describes him thus: "Crosland was evidently a man who never wore his hat on the back of his head, possibly because he had long since lost all hope of wearing a halo. He had a dark, heavy moustache, short side-whiskers, a strong harsh voice with a Lancashire accent, and a truculent blood-shot eye. Everything about him was truculent, in fact; even his nose looked antagonistic to the universe" (*WY*, 13).

Later, when their business and professional relationship has ended, Sassoon runs into the now-mustache-free Crosland in a music hall: "He now looked shrunken, and his expression was lurkingly malevolent" (*WY*, 162). Crosland invites Sassoon to lunch, and it turns out to be an absolutely Dickensian feast. But the enormous meal does not substitute for the fact that Crosland never paid Sassoon the money owed for poems published. It is perhaps too bad that Sassoon chooses never to communicate with Crosland, and they never meet again after the feast, for Crosland is a character worthy of a novel.

Gosse and Marsh are well drawn. Sassoon is grateful to them but also fascinated by their high culture, life-style, and power. W. H. Davies and George Moore come to life in *The Weald of Youth,* as do other literary figures. The finest and fullest sketch, however, is of Helen Wirgman, "Wirgie," who continues in her role as nurturing woman to young Sassoon. She is friend, companion, and surrogate mother to him in London, as "Mamsy" fades into the background. She is also, among other things, a good critic, suggesting, "Wouldn't it be better if I were to put some solid thought into my poems, and go in for more honest everyday words? Somehow she felt that I ought to be writing in a more *physical* way" (*WY*, 29). It is Wirgie who brings about Sassoon's interest in George Meredith that results in Sassoon's writing the Meredith biography in later years.

The Weald of Youth paints Sassoon's nostalgia for his youthful days of great physical activity. Speaking of a racing meet, he says:

The feel of it all comes back to me as though it had happened only yesterday. . . . The mild grey afternoon with its low sagging clouds, the smell of trampled grass, and the clamour of bookies bawling the odds, the yawning intestinal trepidation; and the ebbing aplomb with which I entered the weighing-tent to be jostled by the good-humoured robustness of more experienced riders. And the background of being among a crowd of people, none of whom took more than a casual interest in me as they consulted their race-cards and passed on to have a look at the favourite. An epitome of a young man's existence, one might moralize. Remembering it, I wish that it might happen all over again." (*WY,* 71)

Sassoon the young man comes to life in *The Weald of Youth.* He is diffident, generous, easily awed, and extremely likeable. The idle, privileged Edwardian world of his youth seems ghostly now. One could almost be reading about the eighteenth century instead of the twentieth. But the top-hatted, tail-coated, spatted young gentleman, the youth of the weald, lives on.

Siegfried's Journey 1916–1920

Siegfried's Journey 1916–1920 is the account of Sassoon the soldier-poet. Two years have elapsed since he bicycled off to war at the end of *The Weald of Youth.* Unfortunately Sassoon's early and transforming combat experience, so vital to his development as an artist, must be sought in the last two parts of *Memoirs of a Fox-hunting Man* and the first four of *Memoirs of an Infantry Officer,* fictionalized though those accounts are. Now, in 1916, the reader learns of his growing disillusionment with the war and the development of his epigrammatic poetic technique: "the harsh, peremptory, and colloquial stanzas with a knock-out blow in the last line" (*SJ,* 43).

Written in the darkest days of World War II and treating an earlier wartime and postwar psychological depression, *Siegfried's Journey 1916–1920* is a less satisfactory and satisfying text than *The Old Century and Seven More Years* and *The Weald of Youth.* It especially lacks the feel and love of time and place and the gentle, nostalgic observations that grant charm to the earlier autobiographies. The parade of literary, political, and society figures that marches across the pages reminds the reader that Sassoon had become a celebrity very much interested in other celebrities.

A major weakness in *Siegfried's Journey 1916–1920* is that the text continually refers to *Memoirs of an Infantry Officer* and *Sherston's Progress* in regard to Sassoon's war experience. Sassoon seems to have felt that *The Compete Memoirs of George Sherston,* although fiction or fictionalized autobiography, used up much of the material that should appear, unaltered, in *Siegfried's Journey 1916–1920*. Typically Sassoon says, "My experiences during the next three weeks, which ended in my being sent to a shell-shock hospital, have already been related in *Memoirs of an Infantry Officer.* I am thankful not to be obliged to drag my mind through the details again" (*SJ*, 83). Thus, late in his life compelled once more to remember his soldier side and service days, Sassoon reverts to his alter ego construct, Sherston, to avoid rewriting and thus reliving a period of great physical and psychological suffering: "That inveterate memoirizer George Sherston has already narrated a sequence of infantry experiences—from the end of 1917—which were terminated on July 13th, by a bullet wound in the head. His experiences were mine, so I am spared the effort of describing them" (*SJ*, 103). Concomitantly Sassoon illustrates his development as a soldier-poet encasing his remembrance of horror, pain, anger, and indignation in minisatires, now by depicting the causative events satirically too.

Siegfried's journey winds it way from France to England, to Scotland, back to England, and eventually to America. Home from the front and protesting the war, he is sent to Craiglockhart Hospital near Edinburgh "to recover" from alleged shell shock, the blind to keep the war dissenter out of prison. There, in one of the most moving and significant portions of the autobiography, he meets the then-unknown Wilfred Owen, who shyly offers his poetry to the older, established poet for criticism. Sassoon assumes the role of mentor; Owen, of disciple. Siegfried is characteristically modest in evaluating his substantial influence on Owen:

It has been loosely assumed and stated that Wilfred modelled his war poetry on mine. My only claimable influence was that I stimulated him towards writing with compassionate and challenging realism. . . . Up to a point my admonitions were helpful. My encouragement was opportune, and can claim to have given him a lively incentive during his rapid advance to self-revelation. Meanwhile I seem to hear him laughingly implore me to relax these expository generalizations and recover some of the luminous animation of our intimacy. How about my indirect influence on him? he inquires in his calm velvety voice. Have I forgotten our eager discussion of contemporary poets and the technical dodges which we were ourselves devising? Have I forgotten the simplifying suggestions which emanated from my unsophisticated poetic method? (For my technique was almost elementary compared with his innovating experiments.) Wasn't it after he got to know me that he first began to risk using the colloquialisms which were at that time so frequent in my verses? And didn't I lend him Barbusse's *Le Feu,* which set him alight as no other war book had done? It was indeed one of those situations where imperceptible effects are obtained by people mingling their minds at a favourable moment. (*SJ*, 89–90)

Sassoon was fond of Owen from the moment they met: "I had taken an instinctive liking to him, and felt that I could talk freely" (*SJ*, 87). And Sassoon is able to pinpoint the precise reason for Owen's success: "The clue to his poetic genius was sympathy, not only in his detached visionings of humanity but in all his actions and responses towards individuals" (*SJ*, 91). Owen's biographer John Stallworthy illustrates some of the specific poems Sassoon "corrected" for Owen.[2] The conjunction of Sassoon's causticity and Owen's sympathy formed the creative pool from which emerged the most powerful poetry of World War I.

Siegfried's Journey 1916–1920 depicts Sassoon's emergence as a public figure under the handling of Robert Ross, whom he fondly eulogizes, rendering his fatally ill impresario's farewell: "He said nothing, but took my hand and looked up at me for a long moment. His worn face, grey with exhaustion and ill-health, was beatified by sympathy and affection. The memory of it will always remain with me. How should I forget that look, with what afterwards seemed to have been its presentiment of final farewell?" (*SJ*, 125).

Thomas Hardy is one of Sassoon's heroes in *Siegfried's Journey 1916–1920*. The old writer is portrayed in simple, direct, diary language:

Found little old gentleman in front of fire in candle-lit room. . . . First impression of T.H. was that his voice is worn and slightly discordant, but that was only while he was nervous. Afterwards it was unstrained, gently vivacious, and when he spoke with feeling—finely resonant. Frail and rather wizard-like in the candleshine and dim room, with his large round head, immense brow, and beaky nose, he was not unlike the "Max" caricature, but more bird-like. He knelt by the log fire for a bit, still rather shy . . . quite nimble and not at all like a man of almost eighty. Already I felt at ease with him. . . . T.H. became more lovable all the time. A great and simple man. (*SJ*, 134)

Hardy is somewhat romanticized: an artist transfigured by wisdom, goodness, and honesty into an icon, one who "had written his novels to earn a livelihood" but who now "wrote poetry to please himself" (*SJ*, 136). Yet simultaneously Hardy remains an amicable old man without vanity.

The portraits scroll on in the autobiography, making the text a veritable *Who's Who* of British and American letters; included are John Masefield, John Galsworthy, Noel Coward, James Barrie, the Sitwells, Walter de la Mare, T. E. Lawrence, Robert Frost, Carl Sandburg, Amy Lowell, Vachel Lindsay, S. N. Behrman, Louis Untermeyer, and an especially memorable portrait of Winston Churchill. Sassoon is introduced to the irascible poet laureate Robert Bridges, who "glowered in my direction and gruffly made one of the most surprising remarks I have ever experienced. 'What did you say his name was—Siegfried Digweed?'" (*SJ*, 140). Sassoon had become a celebrity, despite Bridges's remark, a celebrity among celebrities, and a poet politically working the literary establishment to advance his career.

Siegfried's Journey 1916–1920 can be divided into three parts: the last half of World War I and Sassoon's efforts in and against it; his postwar experiments in the socialist camp; and his lecture tour of North America, described with humor and bewilderment.

A more unlikely socialist than Siegfried Sassoon, fox-hunting gentleman, is hard to imagine. Nevertheless Captain Sassoon had cared for his men, and with the war over he cared about the veteran in a society very desirous and willing to forget the sacrifices hundreds of thousands of young people had made for them. Sassoon campaigned for the Labour party in the 1919 election, and he went up to Oxford in an abortive attempt to study economics to aid the socialist cause. Appointed to the literary editorship of the socialist *Daily Herald,* he began to tire of the confrontations and the company. Still a man of action, Sassoon could not abide the slow pace of progress and reform, and his faith in the ability of the working class to effect change for the better quickly eroded. He preferred a vision of a single, peaceful society rather than one in continual class conflict.

Siegfried's Journey 1916–1920 concludes with Sassoon's American adventure. Essentially insular, he is bewildered by the United States. He crossed the Atlantic to read his poetry and to tell America that war does not pay. Americans did not want to hear that message. War seemed to have paid quite well, with the country in the midst of unprecedented prosperity. Publicity embarrassed Sassoon. America's size, variety, and vitality confused and intimidated him. The tour was successful professionally and financially, but America was the future and Sassoon was not sure he wanted to be part of it.

Looking backward, Sassoon treats his younger self in *Siegfried's Journey 1916–1920* like a bemused uncle interrogating a child. It was not within Sassoon to be very censorious of the contemporaries of his youth and the era in which they had intensely lived—except when it came to attitudes about war. One aspect of a young, maturing person's life absent in the autobiographical trilogy is sexual interest and exploration. In respect to sex Thomas Mallow observes that "In both the Sherston memoirs and the autobiographies—all three volumes of each, which take both persona and author past the age of thirty—it is almost eerily absent. Allowing for any standard of reticence, literary or social, its want is conspicuous."[3] Clearly his reluctance to mention passion and sex was because his sexual choice was unacceptable to the general public in his lifetime. Indeed that choice was illegal for most of his days.

Except for sex and for the lack of extensive information about his relationship with his family, Sassoon is thorough and honest in the autobiographical trilogy. The poet does not address psychoanalytic complexities but is instead satisfied with externalities presented on a rich, full, and colorful canvas. Motion is the sure sign of life, and thus Sassoon's long narrative brings his youth back in the imagination, depicting in fine, conversational prose how a simple, sincere, sensitive boy gathered experiences pleasant and terrible to use as grist for the mill of poetry.

In a sense the three autobiographies are about Sassoon's psychological self-preservation, not as texts but as process. They afforded him another opportunity to live in a reconstructed past when the raw present was hard to endure. They are a part of "the literature of survival."[4] Many of the historical unpleasantries of the period covered in the trilogy are ignored: the suffragist movement, the Irish rebellion, the abominable social conditions of the poor.

Nevertheless proportions are right in the trilogy, and the photograph of Sassoon's closed society is sharp, clear, and detailed too. Written for a comfortable middle-class audience wishing to identify with the upper-class life young Siegfried lived, the Sassoon story was a critical and commercial success and, to its credit, it remains popular leisurely reading today.

Chapter Seven

Diarist

Sir Rupert Hart-Davis, the distinguished editor and publisher, as well as Siegfried Sassoon's literary executor, realized that the matrix of his friend's art resided in the experiences recorded in his diaries, written from 1905 to 1956 (*Diaries 1920–1922,* 9). The earlier documents, though incomplete, provide yet another autobiographical narrative of those critical years of war and postwar activities in which Sassoon experienced what became the subject matter of his art, while simultaneously creating that art. Sir Rupert introduced and edited the diaries of 1915–25 in three volumes: *Siegfried Sassoon Diaries 1915–1918* (1983), *Siegfried Sassoon Diaries 1920–1922* (1981), and *Siegfried Sassoon Diaries 1923–1925* (1985). Apparently the diaries for 1918–20 were lost or perhaps not written (Knox, 148). Pre-1915 and post-1925 diaries have not been published.

Diaries are interesting and valuable auxillaries to autobiography and biography. Vera Brittain's World War I diaries, for example, are of immeasurable aid to scholars working on *Testament of Youth.* (And they present a woman's view of the trials of war.) Sassoon's diaries are major resources for future biographers, as they are the bare bones and the architectonics of *The Complete Memoirs of George Sherston* and the autobiographies. Further, they offer, obviously, insights into the composition of Sassoon's poetry.

Siegfried Sassoon Diaries 1915–1918

Not surprisingly *Siegfried Sassoon Diaries 1915–1918* is the most dramatic and moving of the three edited diary volumes. Moreover, Sassoon first wrote or copied many of his war poems into these diaries, and almost 60 are included, some left uncollected for more than 60 years, until Sir Rupert brought out *The War Poems of Siegfried Sassoon* in 1983.

Siegfried Sassoon Diaries 1915–1918 "provide a fine descriptive account of the 1914–1918 war to be read both on historical evidence and as literature."[1] Most of all, however, these diaries are a revealing, powerful, personal account of a cultured nonprofessional's reaction to the bru-

104

talities of soldiering. Sassoon wrote some of these diary entries under the most appalling conditions: between firefights, in trenches, in bunkers, under bombardment, and while in pain at medical evacuation stations. Illumination was often a stub of candle. Hart-Davis notes: "Siegfried's handwriting was always firm and legible, but these diaries were in tiny notebooks, sometimes in pencil, often by the light of a solitary candle in dug-out or billet" (*Diaries 1915–1918,* 10).

Surprisingly these wartime diaries are also a source of information about Sassoon's later religious poetry. Throughout his postwar life, Hart-Davis notes, Sassoon read and reread his diaries (*Diaries 1920–1922,* 10). Thus passages like the following from 1917 provided a memory bank for later philosophical thought and poetic composition:

All my unhappiness and discontent and hatred of war and contempt for the mean ways of men and women and myself seemed so easy to put away and forget: my morbid heresies seemed like a lot of evil books that one might push into a dark shelf to gather dust. And even the ranks of solemn, brooding pines took on a sort of tenderness, and there was a homeliness in the lights of the camp; and I couldn't hear a bugle anywhere.

I think this craving for something homely is a feeling that overcomes all others out here; even my pseudo-cynical heart is beginning to be filled by it. I am not so angry with the world as I was a week ago. (*Diaries 1915–1918,* 135)

The war diaries present a young man determined to fulfill himself as soldier, citizen, and poet. He suffers the loss of friends like David Thomas, and he endures great tribulations at the hands of foe and friend. War does have a way of maturing someone fast, if he or she survives.

Of special interest in these diaries are the number of descriptive nature passages. Of course, the war in the West was fought to a large extent in Picardy, one of the most beautiful, arcadian parts of Europe. Still, Sassoon was able to keep the obscenity of the war separate from the loveliness of nature, realizing that someday nature would heal its man-made wounds and the scars of battle would sink beneath the tide of renewing life: "The stillness of the pine-trees is queer. They stand like blue-green walls fifty or sixty feet high with the white sky beyond and above. They seem to be keeping quite still, waiting for the war to end" (*Diaries 1915–1918,* 134).

Siegfried Sassoon Diaries 1920–1922

Siegfried Sassoon Diaries 1920–1922 portray the hero-poet as celebrity. He is befriended, courted, and flattered, while trying to find time to seek out new subjects and write a different kind of poetry. Despite running with a pride of literary lions, Sassoon is not happy. The diaries are a record of frustration and readjustment blues.

On the surface Sassoon's life is enviable. He has won justified fame for his physical and moral courage. He has independent means to live on comfortably. He can spend a weekend at Max Gate with the Hardys, or converse with H. G. Wells or Arnold Bennett when he wishes. Robert Graves is still his good friend. But Sassoon is trapped in high society's golden cage. Even on a trip to the Continent he is unable or unwilling to escape his circle and his class. Homosexuality does not provide him with long-lasting, satisfying relationships. Old sports friends now seem too shallow. He believes he is wasting time. The diaries are a way of asking himself, Why am I doing all this? Where am I going? A phrase from 1922 sums up much of his feelings: "How trivial it all seems" (*Diaries 1920–1922,* 147). Prophetically, however, Sassoon thinks, "More and more strongly I feel that I am living my life with the object of accumulating material for future writing" (*Diaries 1920–1922,* 279).

Siegfried Sassoon Diaries 1923–1925

Siegfried Sassoon Diaries 1923–1925 portrays the poet's privileged life in the flapper age. He enjoys the thrill and danger of steeplechasing, although he is able to "realize that racing isn't as important as poetry" (*Diaries 1923–1925,* 27). Fox-hunting continues to stir and invigorate Sassoon, until a bad accident puts a hole in his leg and he is unable to hunt, it turns out, for eight years.

The club luncheons, club dinners, dinner parties, and country weekends continue with the rich and famous, powerful and talented. His friends, companions, and patrons include Edmund Gosse, Edward Marsh, Edmund Blunden, Robert Graves (to whom he gives money from time to time to tide him over financial straits), H. G. Wells, Harley Granville-Barker, E. M. Forster, the Hardys, Harold Laski, T. E. Lawrence, William Rothenstein, Ralph Hodgson, Walter de la Mare, Robert Bridges, T. S. Eliot, Herbert and Margot Asquith, Virginia and Leonard Woolf, Lady Ottoline Morrell, and many other establishment types. Sassoon's social whirling in this period is astonishing. These people seem to have lived on top of each other. Gossip fuels relations. Sassoon engages in a childish feud with the Sitwells and genuinely dislikes Osbert and Sacheverell. He cuts them and they torment him whenever possible. Their relationships alternate between cuttings and guarded reconciliations, but they join forces temporarily against the mimicking Noel Coward.

Sassoon makes an extended trip to the Riviera, and then solo tours of a thousand miles of England by car, afterward feeling that "nothing has been achieved except that I need a haircut and have spent fifty pounds" (*Diaries 1923–1925*, 266). The miracle is that Sassoon was able to find time to write at all. Only someone with Sassoon's horsey background could, in 1924, talk about learning the "entrails" of a car, and light a match to see if his gas tank were empty, "causing a short conflagration which singed my right eyebrow" (*Diaries 1923–1925*, 197).

Despite the frenetic activity, Sassoon is lonely. He finds his role at Wierleigh to be that of a revenant. Like Tennyson's Enoch Arden, to whom he likes to refer, Sassoon is forever "coming back from the dead." He sees himself as a peripheral observer, not a part of society. It is a psychological artifact, not an actuality. He suffers from depression until, in 1925, a new lover animates him. Glen Byam Shaw, an actor 18 years his junior, brings Sassoon joy, and the *Siegfried Sassoon Diaries 1923–1925* ends with Sassoon high on love once more.

Almost imperceptibly Sassoon is moving toward a more spiritual existence and an etheric poetic. He does try to think deeply, even if his lifestyle makes it difficult to do so: "While weeding the lawn before dinner, in Elysian weather, I was thinking about Communism. For once in a way I really did seem to be *thinking,* instead of ruminating, meditating, or wool gathering from one reverie to another. But it is all blurred now, after a rich dinner, and champagne, and the small talk of Mrs. Charles Hunter and Madame 'Lala' Vandervelde" (*Diaries 1923–1925*, 263). Still, when faced with an existential argument for despair, Sassoon, aware of the irony of his advocacy, rejoins with this: "'I should *like* to convince you of the existence of the human spirit.' I overheard myself (dizzy with champagne and vociferation) saying with an air of Christlike conviction. What a remark to utter at Ciro's in Monte Carlo!" (*Diaries 1923–1925*, 104). Advocating the existence of the human spirit would become the substance of Sassoon's later poetic.

Siegfried Sassoon's published diaries show a man approaching middle age, still eager for more recognition and fame, growing set in his ways, fighting an existential loneliness, hungry for a deep personal relationship, and as lost as any of "the lost generation." There are many more diaries as yet unpublished. A reader caught up in Sassoon's personal narrative can only hope to read them someday.

Chapter Eight

A Poet's Creed
Aesthetics and Criticism

Siegfried Sassoon was not a major critic, aesthetician, or poetic theorist. His approach to literary postulation was pragmatic. When pressed in an interview or conversation he tended to make conservative observations in which he advocated traditional forms and plain Wordsworthian language. In fact he often contemplated the source of creativity, the essence of poetry, its function in society, and the role of the poet. Basically Sassoon saw himself as a nature poet in the tradition of English romanticism. His artistic values were those of "the great tradition."

Two substantial Sassoon texts present most of his critical theory: *On Poetry* (1939), first delivered as a lecture at the University of Bristol on 16 March 1939, and the biography *Meredith* (1938), in which Sassoon too modestly states that he is "no critic, but a tolerable appreciator... incapable of pouring forth ... penetrative comments."[1]

On Poetry

On Poetry can be seen as a retroactive Shelleyan "A Defence of Poetry," Georgian style. Poets are vital to society, in that they perpetuate the values of the culture. The conservative and traditional Sassoon also sounds like Wordsworth when he tells his audience that we hear the harmonious hymns of being "most through simple and long familiar things—through remembered doings transmuted by memory—and in the recurrence of life-learned experiences."[2] He feels that poetry, uttered inspiration, should be very subjective, centered on such aspects of one's personal life as friendship, small pleasures, observations of nature, and a distillation of accumulated, wisdom-producing experiences. The poet is born; the artist is self-made.

The essay begins with prosody: "The art of poetry is, of course, the development of a tradition of exact and metrical use of language" (*OP,* 6). Thus Sassoon deliberately eliminates many if not most modernist poets from his

108

Parnassus, even though earlier, in *Siegfried's Journey*, Sassoon says, "I have always found prosody a perplexing and unassimilable subject" (*SJ*, 159).

Sassoon shrugs off creativity theory with the dictum that in "inventive genius . . . there is some quality which cannot be explained or analyzed, which transcends artifice and belongs to the secret chemicals of emotional aliveness" (*OP*, 7). Thus inspiration comes out of the brew of emotional life.

The poet argues for simple, direct communication in poetry. Abstraction, expressionism, and obtuse, inaccessible ratiocination make poetry unintelligible and unwanted. A poet moves a reader by speaking directly and by transferring his or her feelings and emotions to a receptive, sympathetic listener. A great poet is most memorable and effective when he or she speaks the simplest language of the heart, but Sassoon is moved and inspired by the metaphysical poets—George Herbert, Henry Vaughan, and John Donne, hardly simple sayers. As other critics have pointed out, the simple language of the heart is not so simple when reception relies on varying interpretations of experience and the gelatinous nature of language. Poets like Pound and Eliot or Auden and Spender are lacking in the simplicity and directness of a Housman. Purposeful ambiguity confuses rather than enriches. Sassoon also opposes deep criticism and the linguistic experiments of poets like Edith Sitwell and Wallace Stevens.

Sassoon has no poetic school or system to propose or defend. His aesthetics render down to personal taste and putative values. His advice to neophyte poets is to think in pictures: "Thinking in pictures is my natural method of self-expression. I have always been a submissively visual writer" (*OP*, 19). Visualizing is first external and then internal. It can be literal or purely imaginative. As to sound: "The ear is not enough" (*OP*, 19). And the mind is second to the heart.

In *On Poetry* Sassoon undertakes a rear-guard holding action against the onslaught of modernist poetry. He makes the impossible attempt to regroup a fragmented art form, just as his conservative compatriots in politics vainly attempted to reassemble a fragmented society.

Meredith

Siegfried Sassoon's biography of George Meredith, his favorite nineteenth-century novelist and poet, is a leisurely, laudatory, missionary study devoid of psychological insights. Sassoon relies on his poet's intuition in his readings of Meredith's work. He also acknowledges a considerable debt to the perceptions of Desmond MacCarthy.[3]

Sassoon feels that Meredith is a poet's novelist, one whose prose is not very different from his poetry, both formed from original metaphor. A particular aspect of Meredith's appeal to Sassoon is what Sassoon perceived as the overriding significance of nature in Meredith's writing. For example, the nature poems "Dirge in the Woods" and "Woodland Peace" evince the "quintessence of Meredith as a nature poet" (M, 105). Nature closely observed and truly depicted is Sassoon's yardstick of literary value. Sassoon thus sums up Meredith: "Most of his finest poems are inspired by the connection of human life and passion with the life of nature, and it is only when they stand in direct contact with nature that the characters in his novels put on their full grandeur and charm" (M, 262). Would not Sassoon have used the same words, justly, had the biography been about Hardy?

Sassoon sticks close to the known facts of Meredith's life, and although he adds little or nothing to biographical knowledge, he skillfully produces a readable narrative that is also personally revealing of Sassoon's predilections in literature.

Predictably Meredith's canonical works receive major attention: *The Ordeal of Richard Feverel, The Egoist,* and *Diana of the Crossways* in the novels; *An Essay on Comedy,* the seminal genre study; and *Modern Love,* the sonnet-narrative rightly regarded by Sassoon as Meredith's "poetic masterpiece" (M, 47). This last work, which clearly influenced Sassoon's short, aggressive war poems, Sassoon cannot praise too highly: "It remains, and will endure, as a great and original poem, an artistic construction of perfect unity" (M, 49).

Sassoon's great interest in and appreciation for Meredith surely stemmed from a combination of several disparate factors—his genuine admiration for Meredith's writing, of course; nostalgia for a Victorian childhood in which he read Meredith with Wirgie; and a temperamental identification as fellow artist: "His temperament was that of a poet and intellectual experimenter. He was always an unwilling novelist, and he became contemptuous of the task of writing fiction for a middle-minded public" (M, 36). Further, Sassoon, now 60, was surely aware that Meredith had had certain experiences similar to his own. Meredith's first marriage was unhappy and ended in permanent separation. He cherished his one son. He was unappreciated in his later years. Sassoon could identify and commiserate.

On the other hand, Meredith appeared to Sassoon to have a vitality he lacked. Thus he remained a disciple: "The idea of Meredith means a sense of being fully alive. To be at one's best is to be Meredithian" (*M*, 263).

The critic Sassoon knows that he is unable to turn the tide of modernism. Trying to do so in 1939 or 1945 would have been ludicrous. Better to state how one feels and show how one works. Better to illustrate what is of continuing literary value through the exemplar of a superior literary artist of the century before.

Chapter Nine

Achievement

First of all, Siegfried Sassoon created a new poetry of war. The most widely read of the soldier-poets of World War I, he broke with the romanticized pictorialization of war as a series of dashing cavalry charges, as in Tennyson's "The Charge of the Light Brigade," and rougher but exotic and distant views of soldiering and battle, like Kipling's *Barrack-Room Ballads.* In Sassoon's insistence on producing images of battle that attempted to shock the British public out of its jingoistic victory lust, he forged a poetry of suffering, pain, and truth that is, surprisingly, a progestational part of modernism. D. J. Enright proposes that Sassoon's war poetry "has a clear right to be considered part and parcel of modern poetry. It would be strange were this not so; for the experience of the War was emphatically one which could not be conveyed in debilitated nineteenth-century poetic conventions.... The style capitulated to the subject matter" (Enright, 162). Violence has turned out to be the systemic experience of the twentieth century and the ultimate subject.

Significantly it was Wilfred Owen who seems to have been the first to recognize the uniqueness of Sassoon's contribution to poetry. In a letter to his mother from Craiglockhart Hospital, written on 15 August 1917, he wrote, "I have just been reading Siegfried Sassoon, and am feeling at a very high pitch of emotion. Nothing like his trench life sketches has ever been written or ever will be written. Shakespere reads vapid after these. Not of course because Sassoon is a greater artist, but because of the subjects, I mean. I think if I had the choice of making friends with Tennyson or with Sassoon I should go to Sassoon.... That is why I have not yet dared to go up to him and parley in a casual way" (Stallworthy, 204). Happily he did dare, the next day. And English poetry must forever be grateful to Sassoon for discovering Wilfred Owen, helping the younger man to find a voice appropriate for the experiences he had had and would have, and encouraging the posthumous publication of Owen's poetry.

Sassoon was also the combat poet most widely read by other soldiers in the war. Thus he influenced Owen, Graves, and almost every other British and American soldier-poet who survived the Somme. His language became the medium of warfare expression because it was so widely

112

imitated and because he sensed that the horrendous conditions and the ultimate shock of 700,000 British men killed could not then "be absorbed except on poetic terms."[1] Sassoon's interpretation of combat thus changed modern English poetry. For Samuel Hynes "The change in Sassoon's rhetoric . . . was a complete one: he began 1916 as one kind of poet and ended the year as an antithetically different kind."[2] The Battle of the Somme in 1916 was therefore the watershed not only for twentieth-century British history but also for modern English poetry. A decade later both the surviving war poets, especially Sassoon, Graves, and Blunden, and the reading public in Britain and America learned how to express and receive the combat experience of the war through the medium of prose.

Oddly, in certain ways Sassoon has, in the last quarter of the twentieth century, been credited with more power than he had. Captious revisionist critics, looking for scapegoats for the decline of British power and the end of the empire, turned to Sassoon, Graves, and other antiwar poets and blamed them, their tocsins, and their supposed lachrymose self-pity for eviscerating British manhood and courage. It is a nonsensical view but interesting in that it establishes the continued regard for Sassoon as a modern poet, if not one central to modernism. Indeed few poets ever seem important enough to blame for the decline of the moral fiber of a race.

Sassoon's sympathy for and focus on the common soldier's suffering, a theme picked up by Owen, prefigures the literature of the enlisted man, a literature that, transposed to America, engendered the great World War II soldier novels like Norman Mailer's *The Naked and the Dead* and James Jones's *From Here to Eternity.*

Sassoon's war poetry was didactic. The poems that attacked the political, church, and military movers and shakers of the war, the civilians who profited by the war or encouraged its continuation out of ignorance, and the shameful, propaganda-mongering journalists who lied about the progress of the war destroyed British complacency and belief that God was on their side, dead soldiers went to a heavenly Valhalla, and the war was worth the cost. Sassoon taught the public, over a 30-year period, that it was not.

The poetry Sassoon wrote during the last 40 years of his life was an anticlimax to his 1916–18 production, a few score poems that earned him a distinguished place in the history of twentieth-century British poetry and, collaterally, in the chronicles of war and antiwar. His poems had an impact on the Thirties Poets: Auden, Spender, MacNeice, and Day Lewis, who, having read his poems in school, absorbed their own pacifism from them. The war poems continue to be anthologized, read, discussed, and quoted.

Sassoon then tried to continue to mine his satiric vein in the service of socialism, but it quickly ran out. Slowly but irrevocably, the needs of his soul gained ascendance over those of his mind and his body, and he turned to religion and religious poetry. The new poems did not find favor with modernist critics or the declining poetry-reading public, but a coterie of aficionados continue to enjoy his modest introspections, his metaphysical explorations, and the delicate tracery of his aging. They find art, beauty, and solace in his spiritual journey.

Sassoon's autobiographical fiction, *The Complete Memoirs of George Sherston,* and his three autobiographies, *The Old Century and Seven More Years, The Weald of Youth,* and *Siegfried's Journey,* were an unhappy man's method of subsuming his personal life and displacing his grief and his love for lost comrades by reliving his earlier life. In doing so he recorded, in delicate, pointed, exquisite prose, some of the best of the between-the-wars period, the bitter life of a citizen-soldier in the first war of industrial civilization, and he created a joyous memoir of late Victorian and Edwardian country life that has given pleasure to three generations of readers. Finally, "Remembering the war became something like a life's work" (Fussell, 92). And he did it brilliantly. In the future as in the past, those who would understand the British and World War I will go to Sassoon and Graves and Blunden, instead of political biographies, regimental histories, and lifeless scholarly analyses.

As a skilled poet, a precise social observer, a war realist, a profound recorder of a great human-made catastrophe, a chronicler of an era and a class, and an aging everyman searching for his lost God in a materialistic world, Sassoon helped to make sense of and reconstruct his broken world and, ultimately, ours.

Siegfried Sassoon was a very crash of binaries: an agnostic-turned-mystic, a Jew and an Englishman, a cynic who believed in angels and ghosts, a soldier-pacifist who won medals for combat bravery, a sensitive poet and a fox-hunter who could have stepped out of a print by Bewick or a story by Surtees. A near-last photo of him, sitting in his "writing chair," shows Squire Sassoon, one-time socialist, now the old cavalier, still wearing knee breeches and long stockings.

Writing of Wilfred Owen some 25 years after his friend's death, Sassoon said, "I am unable to believe that 'whom the gods love die young.' Perhaps the Grecian writer who coined the saying had it in mind to hint that the less men see of life the pleasanter their opinion of it must be. My own conviction is that 'whom the gods love' are allowed to fulfill the early promise of their powers" (*SJ*, 109). Surviving trench warfare, living to old age, honored and respected, his life made full by religion, convinced of an afterlife, Sassoon had reason, at the end, to believe that his God did love him.

Notes and References

Chapter One

1. Stanley Jackson, *The Sassoons* (London: Heinemann, 1968), 1; hereafter cited in text.

2. *The Old Century and Seven More Years* (New York: Viking, 1939), 31–32; hereafter cited in text as *OC*.

3. Letter to D. Felicitas Corrigan, 25 June 1965, in D. Felicitas Corrigan, *Siegfried Sassoon: Poet's Pilgrimage* (London: Victor Gollancz, 1973), 47; hereafter cited in text.

4. *The Weald of Youth* (New York: Viking, 1942), 184; hereafter cited in text as *WY*.

5. Paul Fussell, *The Great War and Modern Memory* (London: Oxford University Press, 1975), 7; hereafter cited in text.

6. Denis Winter, *Death's Men: Soldiers of the Great War* (London: Penguin, 1979), 133.

7. Arthur E. Lane, *An Adequate Response: The War Poetry of Wilfred Owen and Siegfried Sassoon* (Detroit: Wayne State University Press, 1972), 107; hereafter cited in text.

8. Robert Graves, *Good-bye to All That* (London: Jonathan Cape, 1929), 224; hereafter cited in text.

9. *Siegfried Sassoon Diaries 1915–1918,* ed. Rupert Hart-Davis (London: Faber & Faber, 1983), 45; hereafter cited in text as *Diaries 1915–1918.*

10. *Siegfried's Journey 1916–1920* (New York: Viking, 1946), 58; hereafter cited in text as *SJ*.

11. Edmund Blunden, *Undertones of War* (New York: Harcourt, Brace & World, 1928), 169.

12. Harold Owen, *Aftermath* (London: Oxford University Press, 1970), 27.

13. *Siegfried Sassoon Diaries 1920–1922,* ed. Rupert Hart-Davis (London: Faber & Faber, 1981), 73; hereafter cited in text as *Diaries 1920–1922.*

14. *Letters to Max Beerbohm: With a Few Answers* (London: Faber & Faber, 1986), 5–20 passim, and Philip Hoare, *Serious Pleasure: The Life of Stephen Tennant* (London: Hamish Hamilton, 1990), 89–180 passim.

Chapter Two

1. Frank Swinnerton, *The Georgian Literary Scene 1910–1935* (New York: Farrar, Straus, 1935), 14.

2. Geoffrey Keynes, *A Bibliography of Siegfried Sassoon* (London: Rupert Hart-Davis, 1962), 17–34.

3. Michael Thorpe, *Siegfried Sassoon: A Critical Study* (London: Oxford University Press, 1967), 273–86; hereafter cited in text.

4. *Collected Poems 1908–1956* (London: Faber & Faber, 1961), 49; hereafter cited in text as *CP 1908–1956.*

5. Sanford Sternlicht, *John Masefield* (Boston: Twayne, 1977), 59.

6. Joseph Cohen, "The Three Roles of Siegfried Sassoon," *Tulane Studies in English* 7 (1957):180; hereafter cited in text.

7. C. E. Maguire, "Harmony Unheard: The Poetry of Siegfried Sassoon," *Renascence* 11, no. 3 (Spring 1959):116; hereafter cited in text.

8. L. Hugh Moore, Jr., "Siegfried Sassoon and Georgian Realism," *Twentieth Century Literature* 14 (January 1969): 199–209; hereafter cited in text.

Chapter Three

1. Bernard Bergonzi, *Heroes' Twilight: A Study of the Literature of the Great War* (New York: Coward-McCann, 1966), 92; hereafter cited in text.

2. Robert H. Ross, *The Georgian Revolt 1910–1922: Rise and Fall of a Poetic Ideal* (Carbondale: Southern Illinois University Press, 1965), 148–49.

3. John Middleton Murry, "Mr. Sassoon's War Verses," *Nation,* 13 July 1918, reprinted in *The Evolution of an Intellectual* (1920; reprint, Freeport, N.Y.: Books for Libraries, 1967), 70–71; hereafter cited in text.

4. Vivian de S. Pinto, *Crisis in English Poetry 1880–1940* (London: Hutchinson, 1951), 144; hereafter cited in text. Lieutenant Pinto served under Captain Sassoon in the Royal Welch Fusiliers on the western front in 1918.

5. Jon Silkin, *Out of Battle: The Poetry of the Great War* (Oxford, England: Oxford University Press, 1978), 154; hereafter cited in text.

6. *The Old Huntsman and Other Poems* (New York: Dutton, 1918), 8; hereafter cited in text as *OH.*

7. Virginia Woolf, "Old Huntsman," *Times Literary Supplement,* 31 May 1917, 259.

8. Bernard Knox, "Siegfried Sassoon," *Grand Street* 2, no. 4 (Summer 1983):142; hereafter cited in text.

9. John H. Johnston, *English Poetry of the First World War: A Study in the Evolution of Lyric and Narrative Form* (Princeton, N.J.: Princeton University Press, 1964), 86; hereafter cited in text.

10. John Onions, *English Fiction and Drama of the Great War 1918–1939* (New York: St. Martin's, 1990), 43; hereafter cited in text.

11. Fred D. Crawford, *British Poets of the Great War* (Selingsgrove, Pa.: Susquehanna University Press, 1988), 125; hereafter cited in text.

12. John Press, *Poets of World War I* (Windsor, Berkshire, England: Profile Books, 1983), 42; hereafter cited in text.

13. Elaine Showalter, "Rivers and Sassoon: The Inscription of Male Gender Anxieties," in *Behind the Lines: Gender and the Two World Wars,* ed. M. R. Higgonnet (New Haven, Conn.: Yale University Press, 1987), 64.

14. D. J. Enright, "The Literature of the First World War," *The Modern Age* (London: Penguin, 1961), 170; hereafter cited in text.

15. *Counter-Attack and Other Poems* (New York: Dutton, 1918), 9; hereafter cited in text as *C-A*.

16. *Picture-Show* (New York: Dutton, 1920), 10; hereafter cited in text as *P-S*.

17. Howard Sergeant, "Poet of War," *Contemporary Review* 202 (July 1962):39.

18. Louis Untermeyer, "Afterthought," *New Republic,* 3 March 1920, 37.

19. *The War Poems of Siegfried Sassoon* (London: Heinemann, 1919), 67.

20. Rupert Hart-Davis, ed., *The War Poems of Siegfried Sassoon* (London: Faber & Faber, 1983).

Chapter Four

1. "Thoughts on Horses and Hunting," *My First Horse* (London: Peter Lunn, 1947), 14.

2. B. Ifor Evans, *English Literature between the Wars* (London: Methuen, 1948), 103.

3. David Daiches, *Poetry and the Modern World* (Chicago: University of Chicago Press, 1940), 88.

4. *Satirical Poems* (New York: Viking, 1926), 11; hereafter cited in text as *SP*.

5. *Satirical Poems* (London: Heinemann, 1933), 62; hereafter cited in text as *SP33*.

6. Humbert Wolfe, *Notes on English Verse Satire* (London: Hogarth, 1929), 155.

7. *Siegfried Sassoon Diaries 1922–1925,* ed. Rupert Hart-Davis (London: Faber & Faber, 1985), 56; hereafter cited in text as *Diaries 1923–1925*.

8. *The Heart's Journey* (New York: Harper, 1929), 7; hereafter cited in text as *HJ*.

9. *Poems by Pinchbeck Lyre* (London: Duckworth, 1931), 9; hereafter cited in text as *PPL*.

10. *The Road to Ruin* (London: Faber & Faber, 1933), b; hereafter cited in text as *RR*.

11. *Vigils* (New York: Viking, 1936), 2; hereafter cited in text as *V*.

12. Stephen Spender, "Poets of Two Wars," *New Statesman and Nation,* 7 December 1940, 570.

13. *Rhymed Ruminations* (New York: Viking, 1941), 13; hereafter cited in text as *RhR*.

14. "The Poetry of Siegfried Sassoon," *Times Literary Supplement,* 1 November 1947, 564.

15. Peter Levi, "Sassoon at Eighty," *Poetry Review* 5, no. 3 (1966):172.

16. *Sequences* (London: Faber & Faber, 1936), 3; hereafter cited in text as *Se*.

17. *The Path to Peace* (Worcester, England: Stanbrook Abbey Press, 1960), 30; hereafter cited in text as *PP*.

18. *An Octave* (London: Arts Council of Britain, 1966), 7; hereafter cited in text as *O*.

Chapter Five

1. Valentine Cunningham, *British Writers of the Thirties* (New York: Oxford University Press, 1988), 44–45.

2. See F. J. Harvey Darton, *From Surtees to Sassoon: Some English Contrasts (1838–1928)* (London: Morley & Mitchell Kennerley, Jr., 1931).

3. *Memoirs of a Fox-hunting Man*, in *The Memoirs of George Sherston* (Garden City, N.Y.: Doubleday, Doran, 1937), 376; hereafter cited in text as *FHM*.

4. Robert Graves, "The Red-coated Fraternity," *Times Literary Supplement*, 23 February 1929, 704.

5. *Memoirs of an Infantry Officer*, in *The Memoirs of George Sherston* (Garden City, N.Y.: Doubleday, Doran, 1937), 251; hereafter cited in text as *IO*.

6. *Sherston's Progress*, in *The Memoirs of George Sherston* (Garden City, N.Y.: Doubleday, Doran, 1937), 245; hereafter cited in text as *SPr*.

Chapter Six

1. David Garnett, "Current Literature," *New Statesman and Nation*, 17 September 1938, 419.

2. John Stallworthy, *Wilfred Owen* (London: Oxford University Press, 1974), 208–15; hereafter cited in text.

3. Thomas Mallon, "The Great War and Sassoon's Memory," in *Modernism Revisited*, Harvard English Studies 11, ed. Robert Kiely (Cambridge, Mass.: Harvard University Press, 1983), 85.

4. John Hidlebidle, "Neither Worthy nor Capable: The War Memoirs of Graves, Blunden, and Sassoon," in *Modernism Revisited*, Harvard English Studies 11, ed. Robert Kiely (Cambridge, Mass.: Harvard University Press, 1983), 121.

Chapter Seven

1. Christopher Lloyd, review of *Siegfried Sassoon Diaries 1915–1918*, *Review of English Studies* 35, no. 138 (May 1984):263.

Chapter Eight

1. *Meredith* (New York: Viking, 1948), 153; hereafter cited in text as *M*.

2. *On Poetry* (Bristol, England: J. W. Arrowsmith University Press, 1939), 9–10; hereafter cited in text as *OP*.

3. See Desmond MacCarthy, *Portraits* (London: Putnam, 1931), 170–86.

Chapter Nine

1. Jeffrey C. Williams, "The Myth of the Lost Generation: The British War Poets and Their Modern Critics," *Clio: A Journal of Literature, History, and the Philosophy of History* 12, no. 1 (Fall 1982):48.

2. Samuel Hynes, *A War Imagined: The First World War and English Culture* (New York: Atheneum, 1991), 156.

Selected Bibliography

PRIMARY WORKS

Poetry

Poems. London: Privately printed, 1906.
Orpheus in Diloeryium. London: Privately printed, 1908.
Sonnets and Verses. London: Privately printed, 1909.
Sonnets. London: Privately printed, 1909.
Twelve Sonnets. London: Privately printed, 1911.
Poems. London: Privately printed, 1911.
Melodies. London: Privately printed, 1912.
Hyacinth: An Idyll. London: Privately printed, 1912.
An Ode for Music. London: Privately printed, 1912.
The Daffodil Murderer. By Saul Kain [pseud.]:. London: John Richmond, 1913.
Discoveries. London: Privately printed, 1915.
Morning-Glory. London: Privately printed, 1916.
The Old Huntsman and Other Poems. London: Heinemann, 1917. Reprint. New
    York: Dutton, 1918.
Counter-Attack and Other Poems. London: Heinemann, 1918. Reprint. New
    York: Dutton, 1918.
Picture-Show. Cambridge, England: Privately printed, 1919. Reprint (as *Picture-
    Show*). New York: Dutton, 1920.
The War Poems of Siegfried Sassoon. London: Heinemann, 1919.
Recreations. London: Privately printed, 1923.
Lingual Exercises for Advanced Vocabularians. Cambridge, England: Privately
    printed, 1925.
Selected Poems. London: Heinemann, 1925.
Satirical Poems. London: Heinemann, 1926. Reprint. New York: Viking, 1926.
    Reprint (enlarged ed.). London: Heinemann, 1933.
The Heart's Journey. New York: Crosby Gaige; London: Heinemann, 1927.
Poems by Pinchbeck Lyre. London: Duckworth, 1931.
The Road to Ruin. London: Faber & Faber, 1933.
Vigils. London: Privately printed, 1934. Reprint (enlarged ed.). London: Heine-
    mann, 1935. Reprint. New York: Viking, 1936.
Rhymed Ruminations. London: Chiswick, 1939. Reprint (enlarged ed.). London:
    Faber & Faber, 1940. Reprint. New York: Viking, 1941.
Poems Newly Selected 1916–1935. London: Faber & Faber, 1940.

The Flower Show Match and Other Pieces. London: Faber & Faber, 1941.

Collected Poems. London: Faber & Faber, 1947. Reprint. New York: Viking, 1949.

Common Chords. Stanford Dingley, England: Mill House Press, 1950.

Emblems of Experience. Cambridge, England: Rampant Lions Press, 1951.

The Tasking. Privately printed, n.d. Reprint. Cambridge, England: Cambridge University Press, 1954.

Sequences. London: Faber & Faber, 1956. Reprint. New York: Viking, 1957.

Lenten Illuminations. Privately printed, n.d. Reprint. Cambridge, England: Cambridge University Press, 1958.

The Path to Peace. Worcester, England: Stanbrook Abbey Press, 1960.

Collected Poems 1908–1956. London: Faber & Faber, 1961.

An Octave. London: Arts Council of Britain, 1966.

Selected Poems. London: Faber & Faber, 1968. Reprint. Glasgow: R. MacLehose University Press, 1970.

The War Poems of Siegfried Sassoon. Edited by Rupert Hart-Davis. London: Faber & Faber, 1983.

Prose

Memoirs of a Fox-hunting Man. London: Faber & Gwyer, 1928. Reprint. New York: Coward-McCann, 1929.

Memoirs of an Infantry Officer. London: Faber & Faber; New York: Coward-McCann, 1930.

Sherston's Progress. London: Faber & Faber; Garden City, N.Y.: Doubleday, Doran, 1936.

The Complete Memoirs of George Sherston. Garden City, N.Y.: Doubleday, Doran; London (as *The Memoirs of George Sherston*): Faber & Faber, 1937.

The Old Century and Seven More Years. London: Faber & Faber, 1938. Reprint. New York: Viking, 1939.

On Poetry. Bristol, England: J. W. Arrowsmith University Press, 1939.

The Weald of Youth. London: Faber & Faber; New York: Viking, 1942.

Siegfried's Journey 1916–1920. London: Faber & Faber, 1945. Reprint. New York: Viking, 1946.

Meredith. London: Constable; New York: Viking, 1948. Reprint. Port Washington, N.Y.: Kennikat, 1969.

Something about Myself. Worcester, England: Stanbrook Abbey Press, 1966.

Siegfried Sassoon Diaries 1920–1922. Edited by Rupert Hart-Davis. London: Faber & Faber, 1981.

Siegfried Sassoon Diaries 1915–1918. Edited by Rupert Hart-Davis. London: Faber & Faber, 1983.

Siegfried Sassoon's Long Journey: Selections from the Sherston Memoirs. Edited by Paul Fussell. New York: Giniger, with Oxford University Press, 1983.

Siegfried Sassoon Diaries 1923–1925. Edited by Rupert Hart-Davis. London: Faber & Faber, 1985.

Siegfried Sassoon Letters to Max Beerbohm. Edited by Rupert Hart-Davis. London: Faber & Faber, 1986.

SECONDARY WORKS

Bibliography

Keynes, Geoffrey. *A Bibliography of Siegfried Sassoon.* London: Rupert Hart-Davis, 1962. Invaluable research tool. All books and periodical contributions to 1962.

Books and Parts of Books

Bergonzi, Bernard. *Heroes' Twilight: A Study of the Literature of the Great War.* London: Constable, 1965. Reprint. New York: Coward-McCann, 1966. Major comprehensive study of World War I poets, with important chapter on Sassoon.

Corrigan, D. Felicitas. *Siegfried Sassoon: Poet's Pilgrimage.* London: Victor Gollancz, 1973. Letters-structured biography and commentary. Reminiscences and anecdotes. A confusing hagiography.

Crawford, Fred D. *British Poets of the Great War.* Selinsgrove, Pa.: Susquehanna University Press, 1988. Discusses the converging currents of imagism, satire, realism, and the experiences of writers in World War I. Comprehensive annotated bibliography.

Darton, F. J. Harvey. *From Surtees to Sassoon: Some English Contrasts (1838–1928).* London: Morley & Mitchell Kennerley, Jr., 1931. An appreciation of Sassoon as a "countryman" who "never lost that deep sense of English country."

Enright, D. J. "The Literature of the First World War." In *The Modern Age 7,* ed. Boris Ford, 162–77. Harmondsworth, Middlesex, England: 1964. Argues that Sassoon and Owen did not contribute to modernism but nevertheless are a part of modern poetry because of subject matter.

Fleischman, Avron. "The Memoirs of George Sherston." In *Figures of Autobiography: The Language of Self-Writing in Victorian and Modern England,* 337–53. Berkeley, Calif.: University of California Press, 1983. Sees *Memoirs* as Sassoon's allegorical pilgrimage from violence to peace and rebirth as a caring, hoping, believing human being.

Fussell, Paul. *The Great War and Modern Memory.* London: Oxford University Press, 1975. The most important intellectual history of the impact, through the mythologizing of the terrible experience, of World War I on subsequent literary tradition.

Giddings, Robert. *The War Poets.* London: Paul Press, 1986. Reprint. New York: Orion Books, 1988. Coffee-table illustrated history and examples of World War I poetry. Good selections.

Hildebidle, John. "Neither Worthy nor Capable: The War Memoirs of Graves, Blunden, and Sassoon." In *Modernism Reconsidered,* Harvard English Studies 11, ed. Robert Kiely, 101–21. Cambridge, Mass.: Harvard University Press, 1983.

Hynes, Samuel. *A War Imagined: The First World War and English Culture.* New York: Atheneum, 1991. World War I as an event in the imagination and a catalyst for modernism.

Jackson, Stanley. *The Sassoons.* London: Heinemann, 1968. Popular history of Sassoon family from its origins in eighteenth-century Baghdad through modern times.

Johnston, John H. *English Poetry of the First World War: A Study in the Evolution of Lyric and Narrative Form.* Princeton, N.J.: Princeton University Press, 1964. Detailed but somewhat pedestrian study of 10 combat poets, with emphasis on those he considers major: Brooke, Sassoon, Owen, and Rosenberg.

Lane, Arthur E. *An Adequate Response: The War Poetry of Wilfred Owen and Siegfried Sassoon.* Detroit: Wayne State University Press, 1972. Significant study showing how Sassoon and Owen, the two most important World War I poets, relocated poetic value in human action, charging verse with the power of actuality.

Lehmann, John. *The English Poets of the First World War.* New York: Thames & Hudson, 1982. Recent brief overview of soldier-poets.

Mallon, Thomas. "All Souls' Night: Yeats, Sassoon, and the Dead." In *Irish Studies 1,* ed. P. J. Drudy, 85–95. Cambridge: Cambridge University Press, 1980. Despite the obvious contrast between Yeats's modernism and Sassoon's traditionalism, both poets are endowed with the same artistic temperament.

———. "The Great War and Sassoon's Memory." In *Modernism Reconsidered,* Harvard English Studies 11, ed. Robert Kiely, 81–99. Cambridge, Mass.: Harvard University Press, 1983. Psychological study examining Sassoon's use of memory in the Sherston trilogy and the autobiographies. Mallon argues that World War I did not in fact alter Sassoon's personality very much.

Onions, John. *English Fiction and Drama of the Great War 1918–1939.* New York: St. Martin's, 1990. The image of the soldier in the between-the-wars literature, so-called war books.

Press, John. *Poets of World War I.* Windsor, Berkshire, England: Profile Books, 1983. Short, useful overview of British World War I poetry and song. Emphasizes combat poets.

Rogers, Timothy, ed. *Georgian Poetry 1918–1922: The Critical Heritage.* London: Routledge & Kegan Paul, 1977. Useful chronological compendium of 40 years of criticism of the five volumes of Edward Marsh's *Georgian Poetry.* Sassoon was a major contributor to two.

Ross, Robert H. *The Georgian Revolt 1910–1922: Rise and Fall of a Poetic Ideal.* Carbondale: Southern Illinois University Press, 1965. History of the Georgian movement from inception to decline.

Roth, Cecil. *The Sassoon Dynasty.* London: Robert Hale, 1941. Reprint. New York: Arno, 1977. Florid family history. Siegfried receives light treatment, and Roth is inaccurate concerning his writings.

Silkin, Jon. *Out of Battle: The Poetry of the Great War.* Oxford, England: Oxford University Press, 1972. Outstanding critical study of World War I poets, including noncombatants. Faults Sassoon for inability to mesh thought and response.

Swinnerton, Frank. *The Georgian Literary Scene 1910–1935: A Panorama.* London: Hutchinson, 1935; revised ed., 1954. Comprehensive evaluation of Georgian movement. Locates Sassoon's place and contribution.

Thorpe, Michael. *Siegfried Sassoon: A Critical Study.* Oxford, England: Oxford University Press, 1967. Key critical study of Sassoon canon.

Articles

Cohen, Joseph. "The Three Roles of Siegfried Sassoon." *Tulane Studies in English* 7 (1957):169–85. Sees Sassoon as playing three roles in his life: angry prophet, country gentleman, and self-effacing hermit.

Das, Sasibhushan. "War and the Poets; Siegfried Sassoon: The War Poet." *Calcutta Review* 1, n.s. (December 1967):267–93. Argues that Sassoon's war poetry failed to integrate propaganda with his lyrical impulse or to adequately submerge it.

Knox, Bernard. "Siegfried Sassoon." *Grand Street* 2, no. 4 (Summer 1983): 140–51. Interesting personal reflections about growing up in Britain reading Sassoon's poetry and prose between the two world wars. Illustrates Sassoon's impact on the World War II generation.

Levi, Peter. "Sassoon at Eighty." *Poetry Review* 57, no. 3 (Autumn 1966):171–73. Encomium defining Sassoon as a metaphysical poet with a special integrity of style.

Lohf, Kenneth A. "Friends among the Soldier Poets." *Columbia Library Columns* 30 (September 1980):3–18. The influence of Sassoon on Owen, described and evaluated.

Maguire, C. E. "Harmony Unheard: The Poetry of Siegfried Sassoon." *Renascence* 11, no. 3 (Spring 1959):115–24. Careful study of Sassoon's post–World War I poetry, demonstrating the poet's growth, greater control, and philosophical development.

Moore, L. Hugh, Jr. "Siegfried Sassoon and Georgian Realism." *Twentieth Century Literature* 14 (January 1969):199–209. Influence of Georgian movement on Sassoon's poetry. Opposes conventional view that pre–World War I Sassoon poetry is weak.

Sergeant, Howard. "Siegfried Sassoon—Poet of War." *Contemporary Review* 202 (July 1962):37–41. Argues that Sassoon's World War I experiences exhausted his capacity for strong feeling and caused him to turn to history and remembering the dead. Also contains a brief but cogent overview of Sassoon's career as a poet.

Showalter, Elaine. "Rivers and Sassoon: The Inscription of Male Gender Anxieties." In *Behind the Lines: Gender and the Two World Wars,* ed. Margaret Randolph Higonnet, 61–69. New Haven, Conn.: Yale University Press, 1987. Feminist psychoanalytic study of the discourse of shell shock. Argues that Victorian sensibilities were what was shocked. Discusses Sassoon's relationship with his Freudian psychologist, William H. R. Rivers.

Welland, Dennis. "Sassoon on Owen." *Times Literary Supplement,* 31 May 1974, 589–90. Interesting recollection of 1949 interview and correspondence with Sassoon.

Williams, Jeffrey C. "The Myth of the Lost Generation: The British War Poets and Their Modern Critics." *Clio: A Journal of Literature, History and the Philosophy of History* 13, no. 1 (Fall 1982):45–56. An antirevisionist review of the impact of British World War I casualty rates, and the combat poets who deplored them, on subsequent history. Argues that although poetry provided a palatable way for the public to absorb the loss, it did not destroy British character.

Index

129

The Author

Sanford Sternlicht, professor emeritus of theater and English at the State University of New York at Oswego, is currently part-time professor of English at Syracuse University. He is the author of the following books: *Gull's Way* (1961), poetry; *Love in Pompeii* (1967), poetry; *The Black Devil of the Bayous* (1970), history, with E. M. Jameson; *John Webster's Imagery and the Webster Canon* (1972); *McKinley's Bulldog: The Battleship Oregon* (1977), history; *John Masefield* (1977); *C. S. Forester* (1981); *USF Constellation: Yankee Racehorse* (1981), history, with E. M. Jameson; *Padraic Colum* (1985); *John Galsworthy* (1987); *R. F. Delderfield* (1988); *Stevie Smith* (1990); and *Stephen Spender* (1992).

He has edited *Selected Short Stories of Padraic Colum* (1985), *Selected Plays of Padraic Colum* (1986), *Selected Poems of Padraic Colum* (1989), and *In Search of Stevie Smith* (1991). His articles on subjects from Shakespeare to Graham Greene have appeared in numerous journals, and his poetry has appeared in more than 300 publications. He received the *Writer Magazine* New Poets Award in 1960, a poetry fellowship from the Poetry Society of America in 1965, and several State University of New York Research Foundation fellowships and grants.